A Year of Broken Promises

(Book 2 of *An Irish Family Saga*)

Sequel to *'A Pocket Full of Shells'*

By

<u>Jean Reinhardt</u>

Historical Fiction

"The woods are lovely, dark and deep,
But I have promises to keep,
And miles to go before I sleep,
And miles to go before I sleep."

Robert Frost

Copyright

Title book: A Year of Broken Promises

Author book: Jean Reinhardt

Text copyright © 2014 Jean Reinhardt

Cover illustration copyright © 2014 Jean Reinhardt

Self-publishing

jeanreinhardt@yahoo.co.uk

This is a work of fiction; names, characters, places, brands, media and incidents are the product of the author's imagination or are used fictitiously. James, Mary and Catherine McGrother are ancestors of the author, however their story in this book is fictitious.

Author Bio

Jean Reinhardt was born in Louth, grew up in Dublin and lived in Alicante, Spain for almost eight years. With five children and three grandchildren, life is never dull. She now lives in Ireland and loves to read, write, listen to music and spend time with family and friends. When Jean isn't writing she likes to take long walks through the woods and on the beach.

Jean writes poetry, short stories and novels. Her favourite genres are Young Adult and Historical Fiction.

Follow her on:
twitter.com/JeanReinhardt1

Like her on:
www.facebook.com/JeanReinhardtWriter

Join her on:
www.jeanreinhardt.wordpress.com

Other books by the author:

A Pocket Full of Shells (Book 1 of *An Irish Family Saga*)

The Finding Trilogy: a young adult medical thriller series.

Book 1: *Finding Kaden*
Book 2: *Finding Megan*
Book 3: *Finding Henry Brubaker*

In digital and paperback format on Amazon and Smashwords.

For my husband Robbie

and his parents

Harry & Lena

Acknowledgements

I would like to thank the following people for the part they played in the production of this book:

Beta Readers

Pascaline, Brenda, Sharon, Eileen, Christine and Elaine

Cover Image

E.R.Catterson Portraits
Castlederg, Co. Tyrone

www.facebook.com/OldStylePhotographs

(A big thank you to Robyn, who posed so beautifully for the photo).

Noel Sharkey (historian and poet)

The following books proved to be a great source of information in the writing of this story. They are full of well documented events and photographs of people whose families have lived in Blackrock for many generations, including my own:

The Parish of Haggardstown & Blackrock – A History by Noel Sharkey.
First Printed in 2003 by Dundalgan Press (W. Tempest) Ltd., Dundalk.

The Parish of Haggardstown & Blackrock – A Pictorial Record compiled and written by Noel Sharkey, with photos by Owen Byrne.
Printed in 2008 by Dundalgan Press (W. Tempest) Ltd., Dundalk.

CHAPTER ONE

James McGrother hung back from the grave, watching Pat's old shoulders hunch against the wind as he knelt in prayer. Blessing himself quickly before chasing after his three young children, James knew that nothing he could say would lessen his uncle's pain. It was better to leave the grieving man alone, to speak the words in private that he never got the chance to say at the funeral. Earlier that morning, Pat told James he could not face another night without talking to his beloved Annie and had asked his nephew to accompany him to the graveyard.

The young father guessed that his three children were playing hide and seek around the ruin of the old church in the centre of Haggardstown cemetery. The only sound he could hear was the whistling of the wind through the gaps in the broken walls. When he eventually found them, Catherine was sitting on the ground, her arms encircling her two younger siblings. They were leaning against one of the cold stone walls and seemed frozen to the spot. When they saw their father, Thomas aged nine, and his four year old sister Mary-Ann, ran screaming into his arms. James gathered them up and looked over at Catherine, who was smiling sweetly back at him.

"Has your big sister been frightening the life out of ye with her ghost stories again?"

"We made her tell us, Daddy. She said Annie had told her the same story when she was my age and it didn't frighten her at all. Men don't get scared, do they? Does that mean I'm not a man yet?" asked Thomas.

James saw tears well up in his son's eyes and lowered himself until their faces were level with each other. Noting that Mary-Ann was beginning to shiver, he drew her close to his chest and wrapped both sides of his jacket around her thin frame.

"Of course you're a man, Thomas. Aren't you my wee man? Soon you'll be as big as me and then I won't be able to call you that any more. And don't ever be ashamed to say you're afraid. I've been in fear many a time. Ask your mammy."

Catherine had joined Pat at the graveside and James smiled when he saw her patting the hunched back of the elderly fisherman. She rested her head on his shoulder, until Pat laid a hand on the wooden cross that bore his wife's name and hoisted himself up onto a pair of shaky legs. He looked behind to where his nephew stood waiting, before placing his cap back on his head and taking hold of the small cold hand held out to him.

"Is Mamó asleep now? Do you think she's warm enough, Dadó?" asked Catherine.

"Aye, a stór. She's in a safe place and cannot feel the chill of this breeze. Come now, let's get ye all back to the fire and warm up those poor frozen hands and feet," said Pat.

Before leaving, the men took one last look around the cemetery and Pat's eyes came to rest on a plaque that bore the name of a young man.

"Annie reached a good age, James. She lived through some hard times and if I join her tomorrow, I have no regrets. We were given a lot longer than some of these poor souls, like young Doctor Martin over there. Cut down by the fever in his prime he was, while tending the sick and the poor, bless him. He was barely a day over thirty."

"I'm going to be a doctor when I grow up," said Thomas.

James and Pat smiled at the boy who was standing as tall as he could stretch, his chest thrust out. They both knew he would be a fisherman in a few years' time. It was the way things were and they were not likely to change.

The wind had raced ahead to reach the cottage near the shore, where Mary McGrother lay in bed. She was not asleep, but her eyes remained closed as the door opened and a cold draught swept her children into a parlour that was not much warmer than the garden.

"Mary, wake up, you can't sleep all day like this. The fire's almost out and the place is freezing," James scolded as he placed some bricks of turf onto the dying embers.

"Leave her be, son. Leave her be," said Pat.

CHAPTER TWO

Owen McGrother paid close attention, while his eldest daughter read the letter his brother James had sent from Ireland. It was his second time listening to the news being relayed to the rest of the family, gathered in the parlour of his house in Sunderland. Owen placed an arm around the shoulders of his wife Rose, as she sniffed back fresh tears.

"Annie will be sorely missed with a baby on the way and three other wee ones to take care of," said his brother, Peter.

"That's not the worst of it. Read on, love," said Rose.

'We are all missing Aunt Annie and none more so than Uncle Pat. But the one I am more worried about is Mary, she is acting very strangely indeed and has not shed a tear for the woman who has been like a mother to her for more than ten years. She sleeps most of the day and young Catherine is the one looking after the house when myself and Pat are not here. She is not getting to school because of it. I'm sorry to impose by asking for help and I will understand if the answer is no.'

The young girl stopped reading for a few seconds, to look at her aunt Maggie.

'Can Maggie please come and help us out, just until the baby arrives. I think that once Mary has the wee one in her arms it will bring her back to us. If Maggie can come I might be able to go over to ye and work in the quarry, if there are any jobs to be had, as there is very little to be got here. Pat sends his love to all of ye and your wee ones. Your brother, James.'

The room was silent as all eyes turned to Maggie. She shifted in her seat, her mind already made up as to what she would do.

"Well now, all my lot are big and bold enough to take care of themselves. I know wee Jamie comes to my house after work but another hour waiting for a meal from his mother won't kill him, will it Rose?" it was more of a statement than a question.

"Of course it won't. James and Mary need you over there. Remember how you nursed him when he had the melancholia the first time he came over? He needs his big sister to do the same now for his wife. We can help you with the fare and if James comes here he can stay in your house. I'll make sure they all get fed, so you needn't worry about that, Maggie," Rose meant every word.

A letter was immediately written and posted to James the following day.

CHAPTER THREE

A dribble of the broth that Catherine was trying to feed her mother slid down Mary's chin. Neither of them seemed to notice, so James took the bowl from his daughter and said she could go play outside with her brother and sister. Catherine quickly left the house, grateful to her father for taking over a task that had of late, rested mostly on her young shoulders.

"Come on now, love," coaxed James, wiping his wife's mouth, "You need to keep your strength up. I know where you are, Mary. Surely you remember the time I was there myself. It is not a place I would wish on my worst enemy. Come back to us, please. The children need you – I need you."

James looked into the vacant eyes of his young wife. Pat had taken to leaving the house early in the morning, as he could no longer stand to see her wasting away in front of them. The neighbours had stopped calling and even their children rarely played around the house as they used to. A quick knock on the door and a shout for the McGrother children to join them, was the nearest thing to a visit the cottage had received for almost a week, as Mary slowly withdrew more and more each day.

A hundred thoughts and what ifs raced through James's head. What if he had been home when Annie passed away? What if he had stayed in Ireland, instead of spending the last few months in England? They had needed the money, especially with a fourth child on the way. Nobody could blame a father for wanting to look out for his family, for doing his best to provide for them. James was sure that Mary knew how much he wanted to remain at home; fishing and taking work in the harvesting when it was available.

"Surely you can't be blaming me, Mary. *Mary*. MARY," James shouted, hoping to snap her out of her trance.

Catherine ran in from the garden. She had been hovering near the door in case she was needed and heard the shout. Standing in the middle of the parlour she saw tears run down her father's face. She could not recall him ever raising his voice in temper to anyone. Not even to his children on their worst behaviour. It was her mother who had disciplined them and Catherine remembered plenty of times when she felt the sting of her quick hand across the back of her legs.

"Daddy. Daddy," Catherine spoke just above a whisper.

James slowly turned his head towards his eldest child. The look on her face jolted him out of his frustration and he was by her side in two strides, drawing her into his arms.

"I was just trying to get your mammy's attention, love, I'm not mad at her. She's a wee bit lost right now, let's give her some more time, eh?"

With her finger, Catherine traced a wet streak that ran down her father's cheek and into his clipped beard.

"I know, Daddy. I don't mind looking after her until she's better. I'm a big girl now. Aren't I?"

"That you are, my love. That you are. Will you be able to cook that rabbit Pat has skinned, or will I stay and help?"

Catherine felt all grown up shooing her father out of the house, telling him to go tend the nets with his uncle and the other fishermen. The wind was calming down and she knew they would be out in the bay that night. Passing by her mother's bed on her way to the fire, she patted the top of her tangled hair. It had been a week since Mary had let anyone near her with a comb and Catherine made a mental note to try again later that evening. One glance through the tiny window told the young girl her siblings were engrossed in a game of hide and seek with their friends. It wouldn't be long till they were in looking for food so she hurried on with preparing the rabbit, rubbing in the herbs that she had gathered that morning, just as Annie had shown her many a time.

As the men silently worked on their nets, Pat glanced at his nephew and was thankful that in spite of hard times, James had held onto his boat. Some of their neighbours had sold their vessels to feed their families and others had grown too old or too sick to carry on. Hundreds of young people had emigrated from the parish to join family and friends in England, many of them making their way to America from there. They were no longer satisfied with the seasonal work of agricultural labouring or the erratic earnings from fishing, which was always at the mercy of the weather.

"What's on your mind, James? You've been very quiet all day."

"Sure aren't I always quiet. You're not so talkative yourself, Pat."

"Aye, that's true enough, but I don't usually notice the silence lying between us. Today, it feels like a stone wall. Is it Mary you're worrying about? Give her time, she'll be right as rain when the baby comes."

"It's not just Mary. Besides, Maggie will come over and help us out. I'm sure of it," James couldn't look his uncle in the eye and kept his head down as he spoke. "I'm thinking I might have to sell the boat."

The older man stopped what he was doing and stood up, staring in disbelief at his nephew who carried on mending the nets. James could feel the eyes of his uncle on him and was beginning to regret divulging the thoughts that had been tormenting him.

"The last time I felt like roaring at someone was when Annie sold two of her lovely bowls to raise money for Mary's trip to England, that time you were sick. I'll admit, I did let a roar out of me. I never saw Annie jump like she did then, it almost made me laugh," said Pat.

"Well, you can spare me the roar, Pat. I can tell you're not too happy about what I said," James put the net down and looked up at his uncle. "You know that selling this boat is the last thing I want to do but there's work with my brothers in England and every time I spend a few months over, I earn enough to keep a roof over our heads for a good six months. What's the point in holding onto the boat for the seldom it's used anymore?"

"Maybe you shouldn't stay so long away then. You were in England when Mary lost her baby last year and you were there when Annie passed away. We can manage with the fishing and a bit of labouring. I still have some life left in me, don't I? Or am *I* not needed anymore, like your boat, James?"

The younger man was cut to the heart by his uncle's words. He was torn between what he wanted to do and what he needed to do. He had gotten a good run from his boat and it was in fine condition.

"It might not even sell, Pat. It's just something I was considering. Let's leave it for now. I'm sorry about not being here for Annie but even you didn't know how sickly she was till the night she died. If I'd had more warning you know I would have come back straight away."

"Forgive me James. What I said was uncalled for, you don't need me making it harder for you. Myself and Annie were never blessed with our own children to raise. With just the two of us to provide for, I've not had the same worries as you, son, so I'm in no position to give advice. Don't listen to the ramblings of an old man. You must decide what's best for your family, and you will have my blessing on whatever that may be, but promise me you won't act in haste over the boat. Can you leave it for just one more year and then see what must be done. A lot of change can happen in twelve months, James."

"Stop your fretting, old man. I promise I will hold onto the boat for another year. Will that get you off my back now so that I can get on with mending these nets," James pretended to be annoyed.

Pat smiled and slapped his nephew on the head with his cap. He felt blessed to spend his last years with a young man that had become the son he never had. By coming to live with them, James had filled a big hole that had existed for many years in the elderly couple's life together, one that Pat carried the blame for in his heart.

CHAPTER FOUR

The children were asleep in the tiny room above the fireplace. They had gone to bed clutching the presents Maggie brought with her from England. All except Catherine, who had been trying to comb her mother's hair, intent on weaving into it one of the pretty ribbons her aunt had given to her.

"Let me do that, Catherine. Go on up to your bed and have a good night's sleep so you'll be fresh as a daisy in the morning for school."

"Can't I stay home with you, Auntie Maggie? I don't need any more learning, I can read and write well enough now."

"Your father wants you to stay because he left too young himself. Me and my sister would drag him to school until he was eight years old. After that, he got too big and we couldn't carry him. So we would leave him lying in the road because he was making us late for our work up at the big house. He wanted to be with his brothers, out working in the fields and on the farm. As he was the only one in the family who could read, your father felt he had done all the learning he needed and was ready to leave school. Your uncle Owen tried his best to make him go but gave up in the end."

"He never told us that," whispered Catherine.

Maggie looked around the cottage. The men were out fishing and the only other person in the room was Mary, who had not even acknowledged the fact that she had a visitor. It was the perfect opportunity to spend time alone with her sister-in-law.

"That's because he wants you to finish school, my love, even if some of your friends don't," Maggie spoke in the hushed tone of a shared secret. "Your father tells me you already write better than he can. Now don't tell him I told you that. He was always a good reader but struggled with his writing. Sure you only have half a year left to go, that's not long at all. Most of your cousins across the water finished their schooling, a couple of them even got apprenticeships."

Catherine didn't know what apprenticeships meant but it sounded very important to her. She figured a word that long was either something to be ashamed of, or proud of. The beaming smile on her aunt's face told her it was the latter.

"All right so. I'll leave you to look after Mammy. Maybe she'll let you comb the knots out of her hair, she's being good tonight," Catherine kissed the top of her mother's head and hugged her aunt.

When they were alone in the parlour, Maggie took her niece's place at the side of the bed and began combing Mary's long wavy hair. She spoke to her about the children and the baby that was on the way but there was no response from the younger woman. It took all of Maggie's patience to hold back from grabbing her by the shoulders and shaking her. It had been the same with James's sickness. They had all tried to bring him back to them by coaxing, shouting, even slapping him, to no avail. Some of his family had cried in front of him but he never once reached out. It was Mary's visit and the handful of shells his little girl sent over, that finally broke through the invisible wall he had managed to build around himself. Maggie knew she would have to find a way to do the same with Mary, as quickly as possible, before the young woman got too used to her presence.

There was a song that Maggie's mother used to sing to her children as they went to sleep. Maggie often sang it to her own young ones and it was the same piece of music her brother Peter played on his fiddle at the end of family gatherings. She closed her eyes, remembering what it was like lying with her brothers and sisters, listening to the song as they drifted off to sleep. Even the animals at the other end of the cottage would settle down for the night at the soft tones of her mother's voice.

As she gently untangled Mary's hair, Maggie sang *"The Parting Glass."*

> *"Oh all the money that e'er I had*
> *I spent it in good company,*
> *And all the harm that e'er I've done*
> *Alas, it was to none but me.*
> *For all I've done for want of wit*
> *To memory now I can't recall.*
> *So fill to me the parting glass,*
> *Goodnight and joy be with you all."*

As the verse came to an end, Mary crossed her arms over her stomach and curled up in a ball. The comb was caught in her hair and as Maggie was trying to untangle it she heard a soft low moan. It seemed to be coming from across the room, so she peered into the dim light, cast by the fire's dying flames. Thinking that one of the children had crept down the stairs and was hiding in the shadows, Maggie called out in a loud whisper.

"Which of ye is hiding in the corner? Get back up to your bed this minute, do you hear me?"

Mary was still lying in a fetal position and Maggie realized where the sound was coming from. Leaving the comb stuck in the long tresses, she leaned over the younger woman and embraced her, pulling her upright. The two women rocked backward and forward as the song filled the air once more. Huge sobs broke free from Mary's body, drowning out Maggie's voice and alerting the children overhead that something was wrong.

Catherine and her younger siblings were shocked at the scene that met their eyes at the bottom of the stairs. Their mother was kreening and sobbing and their aunt had her clasped in her arms as she sang to her. Both women were slowly rocking to the rhythm of the tune. The children huddled together on the bottom step, waiting anxiously for the singing and crying to come to an end. Gradually, Mary's sobs quietened and Maggie's voice trailed off as the rocking stopped.

"Mary, are you back with us now?" whispered Maggie.

The young mother didn't reply. Instead she turned to look at her three frightened children on the stairs and held her arms out to them. They immediately ran to her, sobbing. After a while, when everyone's strength was spent from crying, Mary kissed her children and sent them back up to bed. She promised to make breakfast for them before they set off for school the following morning.

"Do ye want me to go up with ye?" asked Maggie.

"We'll be grand, Auntie Maggie, sure haven't I been bringing these wee ones to bed for years now?" said Catherine as she pulled her little sister along by the hand.

"I am well able to go to bed by myself," sulked Thomas, ashamed of his swollen red eyes.

"Of course you are, son," said his mother. "Catherine, you settle Mary-Ann while Thomas gets to sleep. You know what men are like if they don't get their rest."

"I do, Mammy. They wake up with faces on them that would sour milk, don't they?" said Catherine.

Thomas didn't care about the disparaging remark from his older sister. His mother had called him a man and that was enough to add two inches to his height as he climbed the stairs.

As soon as they were alone once more, the two women clung to each other and cried fresh tears.

"What brought you back to us, Mary? Was it the song?"

"Oh Maggie, that was my father's favourite song. He would have my mother sing it while he played the tune on his fiddle. It was the last song she ever sang. After my father sold it to pay our rent my mother swore she would never sing again and she kept her word – until the day he left to look for work in Leitrim. He kissed us all goodbye and I watched as my mother took his hand and walked him to the end of the

23

village. I ran around the back of the houses and hid behind a hedge, trying to get as close as I could. She held both of his hands and sang *'The Parting Glass'* to him, and that was the last time I laid eyes on my father.

"You never did find out what became of him, did you Mary?" said Maggie.

"I know in my heart that he's dead," tears streamed down Mary's face as she spoke. "Sure it wasn't too long after he left that we lost my mother to the fever."

Maggie was wondering just how much of the previous two weeks her sister-in-law was aware of. She was afraid to say something that might send the young woman back into the depths of despair.

"Do you remember what happened to Annie?" asked Maggie.

"I do, but I couldn't cry or let myself feel anything. It was as if my heart had turned to stone. I've been aware of James and Pat talking to me and poor Catherine looking after me as if I was a baby. I was afraid to let go, Maggie. It felt as if the loss of my parents, and my younger brother and sisters being brought to America, was all rolled up into the one big pain. I thought that if I was to grieve for Annie, then it would open a floodgate that I might never be able to close. Does that make any sense to you at all?"

Mary's sister-in-law brought her some hot tea and reassured her that what she had experienced was normal, especially for a pregnant woman who had lost so many loved ones.

"I went to see someone in the workhouse back home – just the once, mind you. The old man who used to live across the street from Owen and Rose. Do you recall him?" asked Maggie.

Mary replied that she did, as the image of his thin, crooked frame came to mind.

"Well, the poor old soul spent his last months in there. I saw a lot of unfortunate women in that place with the same look on their faces as you wore, Mary. Many of them had lost husbands and children and had given up on life. I always meant to go back and pay some of them a visit, but I couldn't bear to step foot inside that building. Not even one more time. There are dark places inside our heads just waiting for us to enter. Once you go in, it can be very hard to leave. The longer you stay there, the less likely you are to escape. Promise me, Mary, that you will never go back, no matter how bad things get. Will you do that for me, love?"

As Mary nodded her head the comb swung across her face and she pulled it out from the tangled mass of hair. Maggie took it from her and climbed onto the bed behind the young woman. Easing the wooden teeth through the knots she hummed the tune that had played such a big part in Mary's recovery. When the job was done both women lay down side by side, falling asleep with a blanket draped across themselves.

After a good night's fishing, James arrived home with Pat in the early hours of the morning and knew, as soon as he saw the peaceful expression on his wife's face, that Maggie had worked her magic.

CHAPTER FIVE

The tension that had existed between the two McGrother men dissolved with James's promise to put off selling his boat for one more year. The young fisherman was feeling much more positive as they drew close to shore, having being blessed by two good nights fishing in a row. As the crew of four dragged the vessel along the compacted sand, their wives and daughters gathered to gut and clean the fish. Maggie had turned up in place of Mary and James burst out laughing when he saw her waiting with a large wicker creel at her feet.

"And just what is it that you find so amusing?" she asked, hands on her hips.

"Maggie, I'm sorry for laughing. But you can't seriously hope to carry a heavy creel of fish the two miles to Dundalk. You've grown soft in England these past ten years. The longest distance you have carried anything would be the washing to the clothesline in your back yard – and you're not getting any younger either."

The crowd around them laughed out loud as they carried on with their work. Maggie wasn't sure which infuriated her more, her brother's remarks about her fitness or her age.

"Here, Pat, throw me over those fish you are cleaning and I'll wash them," she said. "Anyone would think I was a gormless fool, the way my *wee* brother talks to me," the *wee* being emphasized for the benefit of the audience.

When the fish were all cleaned and packed into the baskets, each of the women picked one up and headed for the road. James and Maggie were the last two on the beach, Pat and the rest of the men making a hasty retreat. They both reached for the creel at the same time and James got it first. Maggie tried to pull it from him and a tug of war developed between them.

"James, do you mean to walk like a fishwife into town, making a show of yourself?"

"Maggie, who do you think has been bringing the fish in these past two weeks?"

"Well then, why don't we go together? You can take the creel from me if you see me stagger," Maggie was half relieved for his offer. She wasn't sure she would be able to keep up with the other women anyway.

"I'm only thinking of myself, Maggie. Sure by the time you arrive the fish will have tainted and nobody would buy it. The other women would be home and in bed and... oww... that hurt," James rubbed his shin where she had kicked him.

The journey to Dundalk was a mix of pleasure and pain. Pleasure for James to reminisce with his older sister on memories of their childhood in Monaghan. Pain on Maggie's part because she stubbornly refused to hand over the heavy creel to her brother until her back felt as if it was broken.

Early next morning, after another night of fishing, James was surprised to see Mary and Catherine waiting for them on the shore.

"Where's Maggie?"

"Ah, James. The poor woman could hardly stand up straight last night. It's worse she'll be today, sure I hadn't the heart to wake her," said Mary. "Young Catherine here will be a great help, won't you?"

The young girl smiled at her father and hoped he wouldn't mention the fact that it was a school day. Thomas was helping the men with their nets while Mary-Ann picked up a fish every now and then to give it a kiss, which always got a laugh out of those who were busy preparing the catch for market.

"I suppose it won't do any harm to miss one more day of learning, you go with your mammy so. I'll make sure Thomas sets out in good time. Monday morning it's back to school for the week, my girl. Do you hear me?" James used his sternest voice.

Catherine nodded her head and picked up the small creel that Pat had made for her. She always went to Dundalk on Saturday mornings with her mother, even if there was no fish to sell. Going there on a school day made it all the more enjoyable. Sometimes they sold herbs from the plants in the garden, or berries when they were in season, making up for any lack of fish. Catherine loved the buzz of the town and the various sounds it produced. She suspected her mother did too, even though Mary complained about the crowds and the noise to the family, on their return home.

There was a larger than usual gathering of people on the quayside that morning and Catherine asked her mother why so many of them were crying.

"That's Reverend Faulkner's girls being sent to America. He thinks he's doing them a favour by finding them work in the big houses over there. Even though he means well, not all of them young ones will end up in good employment, mark my words," replied Mary.

"Is that the man Daddy says is always taking young girls away?"

"It is, Catherine, and mind you don't get any fancy ideas in your head about following them. There's many a story about bad things happening to those girls, and before they even get off the ship at that."

As they walked back home with the other women, Catherine thought about what her mother had said. Even though her parents were against so many young people leaving home, she had heard others talk about the great life that was waiting for them in America. She wondered what it would be like to sail on a boat so much bigger than her father's and secretly vowed that one day she would find out.

CHAPTER SIX

Young Thomas McGrother sat on the floor near the fire, sulking. He was in no form to play outside with his siblings and their friends. Mary noticed how quiet her son was and left Maggie to settle the latest arrival to the family.

"What ails you, son? You've been sourly all week, you should be out in the fresh spring air with your sisters," said Mary.

"Why do you keep having girls, don't you and Daddy like boys anymore?" Thomas immediately regretted speaking out, afraid of what the answer might be.

Mary tried not to laugh. Her son was clearly not impressed by the arrival of his little sister, Brigid. She felt relieved at the reason he gave for his sullenness. The fact that she and her husband had been through bouts of depression, made her worry that they might have passed something on to their children. Mary knew of families where that had been the case.

"Ahh, son. Is that all that's wrong with you? We have to accept what God gives us, it's he who decides whether we have a boy or a girl. The fact that he sent us another girl must mean that he thinks you're a great fella altogether, helping your father look after a house full of women."

Thomas's face brightened a little, "I would have liked a brother, Mammy. Could you ask God to send us one next time?"

Mary assured him that she would pray hard for his wish to be fulfilled.

"Go on now, off with you. There's talk of a bad storm coming and we could be shut up in the house tomorrow, so make the most of a dry day."

Maggie smiled at the conversation she had just overheard. The baby was asleep and it wouldn't be long before the men returned from work.

James was known for building a good wall, he had learned a lot from helping Mary's father, a stonemason, when they lived in Monaghan. Whenever he was asked to repair some old walls, even though the pay was only for one man's work, James would ask his uncle to help him with the job.

Ever since Annie had passed away, Pat had seemed lost and James would often find him looking into the distance. He seemed to be searching for something but when questioned, Pat would blink and shake his head and the faraway look in his eyes would be gone. It was as they were returning home, having spent the day working at one of the big estate houses, that James decided to broach the subject of his uncle's absentmindedness.

"Have you been listening to a word I've said, or are you off daydreaming again?" asked James.

"Watch your tongue and show a bit of respect. Daydreaming's for women. Did you ever think that I might just want a bit of peace and quiet now and again? It's easier for me to turn a deaf ear than to try and get you to close that gob of yours."

It wasn't the words his uncle spoke that stopped James in his tracks, but the tone of his voice. As he stood watching Pat striding ahead of him, he began to think he had imagined the harshness and irritation that had come out of the normally kind and soft spoken man. A chilling breeze came from nowhere and whipped around the young fisherman. James ran to catch up with his uncle, who had continued walking at a fast pace and not once looked back at him.

"The wind is starting to bite, Pat, would you not put your jacket on?"

"You're getting soft in your old age, son. You need to spend more time out on that boat of yours and toughen up a bit," replied Pat in a much friendlier voice.

The older man adjusted his rolled up jacket, wedged securely under his armpit. James pulled his own tightly around him to keep out the cold draught that was forcing its way under his loosely fitting clothes. Noting the extra space inside his jacket, James realized he had lost a fair bit of weight over the winter. He was a man of slim build and couldn't afford to drop too many pounds without appearing gaunt. In a line up for work, only the strongest and healthiest looking men were chosen and James had spent the winter at home instead of taking up the work his brothers had found him in England. He needed to take whatever labour he could get locally. Unfortunately, this meant that he sometimes missed going out on his boat when the fishing was good. His crew would take it into the bay without him and although he got a small share of the catch, it usually wasn't enough to sell.

Money was scarce with an extra mouth to feed and James had caught Maggie putting food from her plate onto his wife's when she wasn't looking. When he confronted his sister about it she told him Mary needed it more, with a baby at the breast. "Besides, it doesn't do for a middle aged widow to carry too much weight on her. Some handsome prospect might be put off asking for my hand if I'm not careful," Maggie had joked.

By the time Pat and James had reached the cottage the wind was blowing a gale. The women had brought the hens in early and locked them into their coop, under the large wooden dresser that Pat had made for Annie many years before. As he passed it by, he ran his fingers over one of the smooth wooden bowls that had been his wife's pride and joy. A flash of anger surged through Pat at the thought of Annie being forced to sell two of them, but in an instant the feeling was gone and the increased pitch of the wind outside caught his attention.

"There'll be no fishing for a while, James, that storm is settling in, mark my words."

"I think you're right Uncle Pat, it was good that we got that last bit of work."

As the family sat around the table, talking to each other above the howling gale, they had no way of knowing just how prophetic Pat's words had been.

CHAPTER SEVEN

An urgent knocking on the door woke the McGrother household, including the children, all except Pat. James noted that fact as he passed the old man, lying fast asleep on the settle bed in the corner of the parlour. When the door was opened, a young man from the village was swept in by a strong gale that had been blowing continuously for five days.

"Joseph, what brings you out in such weather, has somebody died?"

"No, James not yet, but that may change by morning," the young man replied after catching his breath. "I ran against that wind all the way here. Have you ever seen anything like it in your life?"

"I've never seen a storm to hold onto its strength for so long in my lifetime, that's for sure," said Pat, who had come to stand beside his nephew, one of the children in his arms. "I'm not losing any sleep over it, though. It was young Mary-Ann here that woke me, jumping all over my old bones."

"Sorry to wake you all up but my brother thought you should know that George Elphinstone and James Crosbey are going back for another attempt at rescuing the crew off the *Mary Stoddart*."

He was referring to a low hulled barque that had broken anchor in Dundalk Bay and run aground between Soldier's Point and Blackrock.

"Are they insane? They nearly lost their boats and their lives the last time," cried Mary. "James McGrother, don't you dare even think

34

about joining them while this storm is still raging."

"They won't be in their own boats. They are piloting two vessels from Dundalk with Captains Hinds and Kelly and setting out from Soldier's Point at dawn. The crew has already been chosen, Mrs. McGrother," the young man said.

"Mary, if anything goes wrong and I can help, you know I will," James turned to his uncle. "Pat, take your coat off. If you get blown over I can't stop to pick you up. Be sensible and act your age, man."

The words were not spoken in anger but in a steady, even voice. James did not want to hurt his uncle's feelings but there was no time for reasoning with the old fisherman. As he followed Joseph outside into the storm, James avoided looking at the faces of the two people he knew he had greatly upset – his wife and his uncle.

Maggie tried to lighten the mood as the family sat around the parlour, tense and anxious. Even the children were quiet.

"Why don't I tell ye a story and settle ye back into bed?"

"Go on, children. Do as Auntie Maggie says, I promise to wake you if there's any news," said Mary, who was rocking her baby back to sleep.

When they were alone, with only the sound of the wind encircling the cottage, Mary took hold of Pat's hand, its skin rough and calloused from a lifetime of fishing.

"James didn't mean to chastise you, Pat. He has been concerned about you lately, we all have."

Pat didn't speak, but placed his other hand over Mary's and patted it. The old man was quiet for a while, his head bent. Mary thought he might have fallen asleep sitting beside her, but when she went to draw her hand away he gripped on tight and wouldn't let go.

"Pat, what's wrong? Are you still upset by what James said?"

"Mary, do you believe me when I say, that aside from a wee bit of poaching, I have never stolen a thing in my life?"

"Of course I do. Sure you're as honest as the day is long. What's brought this on?"

"I've done a terrible thing and I don't know how to make amends, without bringing a heap of trouble upon us," Pat was getting more distressed by the minute.

"You can tell me and if you want it kept secret, then I won't breathe a word to a soul. What is it that's bothering you, Pat?" Mary felt sure that it had to be something very insignificant.

The old man walked over to where he slept, and took his rolled up jacket from under the straw filled sack that served as a mattress. When he handed it to Mary she could feel that it covered something solid and heavy. As she lifted up the jacket to let it unroll, two of Annie's wooden bowls landed on her lap. Mary's eyes quickly scanned the dresser and she saw that the four remaining bowls from the original set of six were still there.

"Oh, Pat. Where did you get these from? Please tell me you didn't steal them."

The old fisherman was distraught as he paced back and forth in front of the fireplace, wringing his hands. Mary could see his anxiety rising with each footstep he took and she led him back to the bench, sitting him down gently but firmly.

"Now, Uncle Pat. Calm yourself down, take a deep breath and tell me how you came to be in possession of those two bowls," Mary sat beside the distressed man and held his hand once more.

"James asked me to go collect his wage for the day's work from the big house. You know how he has an arrangement to be paid daily, though how he managed that, I'll never know. He must . . ."

"Pat, stay with me now. Never mind the '*arrangement*' and tell me about the bowls," Mary knew how easily the old man's mind could stray.

"The bowls? Annie's bowls? Oh Mary, I've done a terrible thing," Pat had begun to wring his hands again as he raised himself up from the bench.

"Sit down, will you," Mary's patience was wearing thin. "Tell me what happened when you went up to the kitchen to collect the money for James."

The sharpness in the young woman's voice brought Pat to his senses. He looked at the bowls sitting on the table where Mary had placed them and they seemed to stare back at him, like two accusing eyes. As his head cleared Pat lowered himself onto the seat beside Mary. He told her the cook at the big house had said he should step inside as the weather was turning cold but the heat in the kitchen made him feel uncomfortable.

"So as soon as she left, I removed my jacket to cool myself down. A small dog had come in from the cold alongside me and I hadn't paid much heed to it, but finding myself alone in the kitchen I began to look around. That was when I heard a noise and turned to see the dog's head stuck into one of Annie's bowls," Pat was becoming more agitated. "Oh Mary, what have I done, what have I done?"

Mary could guess what happened next. The sight of a dog eating out of Annie's beloved bowls, a family heirloom passed on to her by her mother, would have been enough to send Pat over the edge.

"Do you think anyone saw you take the bowls? No, I don't suppose they did, else we would have found out by now," Mary answered her own question. "Listen to me, Pat. If they allow an animal eat out of those bowls then they must not deem them of any value. Maybe they'll think the dog ran off with them. Why, that's it, Pat, they'll wonder where they have disappeared to and then replace them with two more bowls."

"But it was wrong of me to take them. I should have offered to pay for them, I just wasn't thinking straight. As soon as I had them rolled into my jacket, I regretted what I had done, but before I had a chance to put them back one of the maids came into the kitchen with money from the Master.

When I got back to James, he was putting the last few stones in place. I couldn't tell him, Mary. I tried but the words just wouldn't come."

"Stop your fretting. I know exactly what we'll do, but James has to be told. We need his help with this. He can put them in one of the sheds or somewhere about the farm and when they are found the mystery of the missing bowls will be solved. Everyone will think the dog had run off with them."

"I can do that, Mary. Please don't tell James about this, it's bad enough that you know, I feel ashamed of myself – and rightly so."

The look of shame on Pat's face combined with the pleading in his voice was enough to convince Mary she should spare the old man any more embarrassment and distress. Patting the back of his hand as she stood up from the bench, Mary promised not to say a word to James – something she would deeply regret in the days to come.

CHAPTER EIGHT

The crew of the *Mary Stoddart* had tied themselves in the rigging of the stricken vessel, her decks being as much as three feet below the level of the high tide. The rescue attempts, though courageous, where in vain against such a raging sea. It was not until the storm had somewhat abated that the ten surviving crew could be brought off the ship. Three of them had been washed away to their death and two had died from exposure while on board.

The boat that James Kelly, Captain of the *'Pride of Ireland,'* had been in charge of was overturned by a monstrous wave. The crew clung to the vessel in desperation and as another wave righted it, they managed to get aboard, all except Captain Kelly. He was swept away as the men watched on, unable to reach him. They heard him shout above the wind, "Lord have mercy on me," just before he was swallowed by the raging sea.

By the time the exhausted and frozen crew reached the shore at Blackrock two local fishermen were dead, James Murphy and Gerard Hughes. A third man, James Crosbey, died shortly afterwards. The tragedy and loss of men, both local and strangers, left a sombre atmosphere in its wake. It was the main topic of conversation, particularly the demise of James Crosbey, who along with George Elphinstone, had saved the crews of two other ships a few years previously.

Although Mary had made a promise to Pat not to tell James about the stolen bowls, she felt it was only a matter of time before he found out anyway. It was important to choose the right moment and she decided to wait until after the funerals of the local men had taken place. James would be angry with his uncle at first, then his compassion would take over, and Mary knew he would handle the problem in a sympathetic manner. In spite of the fact that Annie's bowls were treasured by her family, they were of little monetary value. Even if Pat had been caught red handed with them, a small fine would have been the harshest outcome.

While Mary waited to share the secret with James, Pat had taken it upon himself to leave the bowls behind a shed that stood not too far from the big house. If anyone came upon him and questioned his reason for being on the grounds, Pat had a story ready about losing his cap the last time he had worked on the wall there with James. There wasn't a soul to be seen as he quickly took the bowls from his rolled up jacket and kissed each one, before placing them in the long grass by a wall at the back of the shed. Congratulating himself on his accomplishment, Pat, in his hurry away, never spotted the movement of someone watching him from behind a hedge. He walked as quickly as his old legs would carry him, back to a quiet and contemplative household.

"Where did you disappear to this morning after the funeral? You had us worried sick about you," asked James.

"Can a man not take a walk now, to stretch his legs?" Pat replied.

"And where did your legs take you this past FOUR HOURS, if you don't mind telling us?" James was losing his patience.

41

"Well now, nephew, I DO mind telling you."

Maggie dished up a bowl of soup that had been saved for his return. She called Pat over to the table, hoping to deflect the argument that hung in the air ready to suck the men into another debate about the older man's age and health.

"Such a terrible loss, all those men and young boys gone. Their poor families, my heart goes out to them," Mary said.

The men took the hint from the women and put aside their differences. As Pat raised the bowl to his mouth the door opened and Thomas walked in, having been sent out to search for the old fisherman.

"The Carrolls saw Dadó out by the . . . Oh, you're home," the boy exclaimed.

Pat glared at James and from the look on the men's faces Mary knew an argument was about to be unleashed. She draped a blanket around her shoulders and took her husband by the hand, dragging him towards the door.

"I need to speak with you, James McGrother, outside."

As they walked in the cool breeze Mary shared Pat's secret about Annie's bowls. James was very quiet as he listened to how distraught his uncle had been over the incident.

"I knew as soon as we noticed his absence that he had gone to return them. Don't be angry with him, James. The man has his pride, you should be able to understand that."

"I'm not angry, Mary, I'm worried. He hasn't been himself for a long time now. I've seen it before, some people become a danger to themselves with age. What if he gets injured out

42

chasing rabbits? I cannot bring him on the boat anymore, either. The men refuse to go out with him and I don't blame them. We have to prepare ourselves for the worst, Mary. Pat might soon need to be in a place that he cannot escape from."

"We're not sending him into the workhouse, if that's what you're thinking. If I have to tie him to my wrist like a child, I will, before I'll let him go to a place like that. Do you hear what I'm saying?"

Mary had stopped walking and was looking out over a rough sea. There had been no fishing for a week because of the continuous storms battering the coast and James had not earned anything in that time. She was thinking of the little money they had left when she felt strong hands grip her shoulders.

"Do you think I would do that to any of my family? Besides, the walls around the workhouse were put there to keep people out, not in. I was thinking of the asylum in Dublin," said James.

Mary pulled away from her husband, even more shocked. Hot tears stung her eyes in the cold air and rolled down her cheeks.

"The lunatic asylum? Is that where you would have a member of your family sent? God forbid I ever get old and forgetful."

"He could get help there, Mary. They have the best treatment. All we would need is a doctor's letter and a recommendation of his good standing in the community. If we get those he might be taken in as a charity case. They do it all the time now. He could get the same treatment as the gentry do. Sure wouldn't that be grand altogether?" James almost believed what he was saying. Mary didn't.

"Chance would be a fine thing, I'm sure. I know you mean well, James, but he is not a danger to himself nor anyone else yet. Let's not talk about this anymore, unless Pat gets a lot worse. I promise, I will listen to you then," Mary's voice was a lot calmer.

James nodded and shivered in his light jacket against the cold. He regretted not putting on his heavy coat. Mary saw how chilled he had become and stretched out her arms, offering to share her blanket with him. The walk home was silent but congenial and as they neared their cottage, Pat's laughter could be heard above the children's playful screeches.

CHAPTER NINE

As the sun was sinking in a cloudless sky, James put the last stone in place before heading up to the big house to collect his money. Pat was about to accompany him, but James asked him to wait by the freshly repaired wall, reminding him of the incident with Annie's bowls. The old man shrugged his shoulders, denying any recollection of the event.

Walking around to the back of the large house, James mulled over Pat's denial about what he had done. He was not sure if his uncle was being genuinely absent-minded, or just pretending.

"That was a fierce wind altogether, blowing over trees and knocking down walls, wasn't it? The Master says you made a grand job of the repairs, McGrother. He asked me to convey his appreciation and says he will highly recommend you," the butler smiled, handing over the day's wage.

"Thank you kindly, I would be glad of the mention. I'm not one to refuse work," said James.

As he was putting his cap back on his head before leaving the warm kitchen, the cook picked up from the floor an old chipped dish. She filled it with scraps for the little terrier that had been patiently waiting at her feet, wagging his tail and licking his lips.

"You didn't happen upon a couple of old wooden bowls anywhere in the grounds, did you, Mister McGrother?" she asked. "I think this young scamp here must have run off with them."

James shook his head and smiled. Mary had been right in assuming the dog would be blamed for the missing bowls. He was congratulating himself on having such a clever wife as he approached his uncle, who was walking around a bush, scratching his short, white beard.

"What have you lost now, Uncle Pat?"

"My jacket. I could have sworn I left it across the wall, just there," the old fisherman answered.

"You did, right beside mine," said James as he lifted his own one from the newly repaired stonework.

James looked around the shrubbery as he walked along the hedgerow. Nearing the entrance to a field, he saw the missing jacket draped across an old wooden gate. A large shire horse lifted his head to snort at the young man. James patted its long muscular neck as he called out to his uncle.

"You must have paid a visit to old Sergeant here and left your jacket on the gate. You're lucky he didn't eat it," laughed James as the elderly man walked past him

"Oh, of course, now I remember," Pat was puzzled but didn't let on.

As he was putting on his jacket, he felt something inside the lining and discerned by the shape that it was a piece of cutlery. Not wanting to admit his confusion to his nephew, Pat remained silent as they left the grounds of the estate.

The men walked at an easy pace and as they turned into the road for home, James noticed a carriage parked near his cottage. Two constables stood up from the wall they had been sitting on when they saw the men of the house approaching, while two more came from the other end of the road. James and Pat stopped in front of them as Mary opened the door.

"They've been waiting here for the past half an hour for you James. They've pulled the place apart searching for something and would not let me send one of the children up for you. None of us or our neighbours have been allowed to leave our homes. Now will ye tell us what your business is with our family?" she said impatiently.

"Evening, men," greeted the older constable, ignoring Mary. "Would you mind answering a couple of questions?"

James and Pat removed their caps and nodded their heads.

"Why don't we step inside, out of the gaze of prying eyes?" the older constable suggested.

He signalled to two of his men to remain outside and brought one of them with him. Once inside, away from the gathering neighbours, Mary offered to make tea. The constable declined and got straight to the point.

"Have you come from repairing a wall in the grounds of Freemont House?"

James said he had and that his uncle had accompanied him to help speed up the work.

"I would be much obliged if you would both remove your jackets and hand them over," the constable said, nodding to his young companion.

James had reasoned that four constables and a carriage would never be sent on account of two old wooden bowls. He did as he was asked, without questioning, but Pat took a few steps backwards.

"Uncle Pat, what has you so flustered? Give them your jacket."

James turned to look at the two policemen. "What's this all about, anyway? What are ye looking for? I earned that money in my pocket."

"It's not money we're searching for, McGrother," the older constable said to James. He then turned to Pat and spoke in a much softer voice, "Come on now, be a good man and hand over your jacket. Don't force us to take it from you."

"I'm cold, something ails me. I should lie down for a while. Can ye come back later, when I've rested a bit?" Pat was walking towards his bed in the corner of the room, folding his jacket tightly around his body.

Before he had made it across the parlour, the two constables were upon him. One held onto his arms while the other tugged at the collar of his jacket. Young Thomas raced to Pat's rescue and wrapped his arms firmly around the leg of one of the policemen. James was beside them in an instant, having seen the panic in his uncle's eyes.

"Leave him be, for pity's sake, he's an old man," James said as he peeled his son from the constable's leg.

The men released Pat but stood close to him as James turned his uncle to face him.

"It's me. James, your nephew. Look at me, Uncle Pat. That's better," the elderly man was beginning to calm down and James turned him around once more.

"Here, let me help you remove your jacket. The fire is blazing, sure it's like a furnace in here, isn't it?" James spoke in a soft voice and signalled to Mary.

Pat allowed himself to be guided to the wooden bench at the table in the centre of the room, and Mary sat down beside him, taking hold of his hand.

James felt something solid inside the jacket and frowned as he handed it over to the younger constable, who also noted the object. He rummaged through the pockets but finding them empty, began to inspect the seams. Just under the armpit was a hole large enough for his hand to fit through and when he withdrew it he was clutching a silver teaspoon. The cottage itself seemed to gasp at the sight, as did those who were gathered in the garden outside. The scene taking place in the McGrother house was being relayed to the neighbours by a child looking in through the window. The two constables outside where flanking the open door and wore a blank expression on their faces, acutely aware of how tense the people surrounding them had become.

"I'm afraid you will both have to come with us. That item was reported missing this afternoon," the older constable said.

Mary had pushed herself in between James and the man who was leading him by the arm towards the door.

"Tell your wife not to make this any worse than is necessary. Do you want your children to spend the next few days without a mother or a father to care for them?"

"Mary, move aside. These men are only carrying out their duty, they will soon find out this has all been a big mistake. Go on now love, you're frightening the children," James kissed her forehead.

The constables left the cottage, to be joined by their two colleagues. James and Pat were escorted from their home with a policeman on each side, one hand holding onto their prisoners and the other resting on their batons. They had to push their way through the muttering crowd standing between them and the carriage they had arrived in. It looked to James as if the whole village had gathered, not out of curiosity but to show support for his family.

A low disgruntled hum came from his neighbours and James was afraid some of the younger men among them might do something in protest. Sitting next to his uncle in the carriage, as his wrists were being shackled, James leaned his head towards the window and shouted out to the crowd.

"Go on home, all of you. I know you mean well, but we don't want any trouble. We have done nothing wrong and this will all be sorted out in no time."

As the carriage was pulling away, a few stones could be heard bouncing off the back of it.

"That was the sensible thing to say, young man. Things could easily have turned nasty back there. It's the reason we didn't put these on you before leaving your house. The sight of a man's shackled hands can have a strong effect on his friends."

"I didn't do it for you, constable. I was more concerned about my family and my neighbours," James looked at his uncle as he spoke. "Is it necessary to have manacles on an old man? Can you not see how distressed he is?"

Pat was talking incoherently to himself while waving his hands at something only he could see. Although the constables had not answered his question, James took note of their sympathetic expressions as they sat facing him.

"If you knew our family you would never have put these irons on our wrists. You can rest assured neither of us will be the cause of any trouble for ye."

"You know very well that a constable is never assigned to his own county and we're not left in one place long enough to become too friendly with the locals. There would be little chance of any of us knowing your family too well," the older policeman said. "I'm sorry, McGrother, your uncle seems harmless enough but we have our orders and all prisoners must be restrained – old or young. I suggest you try and talk some sense into the old man before the head constable sees him, some prisoners have been known to act the lunatic, hoping for a more lenient sentence. He might not be as sympathetic as we are."

"I've never seen him this bad," James was at a loss as to what he should say to Pat. "I fear this has all been too much for him to bear. He has been in a fragile state of mind this past few years but more so since the death of his wife."

Pat continued his mutterings, ignoring any attempt James made to reach him. It was in

that sorry condition that the elderly fisherman
was left in a cell in Dundalk jail, separated from
his nephew and shackled to a wall.

CHAPTER TEN

The parish priest walked out of the McGrother house, leaving behind a disappointed family looking helplessly at each other. He had apologized for not being able to bring them any news of their men, except that they were being been reasonably well fed but kept apart. He assured them that the head constable had appeared sympathetic, particularly on account of Pat's age. Unfortunately, the police could not divulge any information about the case, even to a man of the cloth, as they were still gathering evidence.

"This has nothing to do with those wooden bowls, Mary. It's the silver spoon that's caused all the fuss. I hope Pat doesn't talk about taking the bowls, it will only convince them of his guilt," Maggie clucked her tongue as she dished up some food.

Mary was feeding the baby and staring into the fire while her sister-in-law bustled around the table, settling the children. She had been trying to remember all of the occasions when Pat had been missing over the past few weeks.

"Do you mean to say you believe Pat stole that teaspoon?" asked Mary.

"Well, not exactly. More like he was confused and put it in his pocket without realizing what he was doing. I'm sure the magistrate will take his age into account."

"It was concealed in the lining of his jacket, Maggie. Nobody slips something that size easily into their clothing in a moment of confusion. I cannot believe he would do a thing like that. Pat is as honest as the day is long."

"Why would the big house make such a fuss over one wee spoon anyway?" asked Catherine in between gulps of broth.

The two women exchanged glances. The same thought had entered their heads but neither had wanted to voice it. James and his uncle had been held for twenty four hours and only their priest had been allowed in to see them. Even he could not find out what all the fuss was about.

"I am going into town tomorrow and if I have to stay outside that prison for a week, I will, until someone tells me what is going on."

"I'll come with you, Mary. We can get young Rosie Matthews to look after the wee ones while we are gone," said Maggie.

The children protested that they too wanted to see their father and Pat, but the women ignored the fuss they were making and sent them outside so they could talk in peace. The baby would have to go with them to town, as she was still at the breast and they would need to bring enough food for a couple of days wait. Maggie put some eggs on the boil while Mary gathered what she would need for swaddling Brigid and keeping her warm.

Next day, hardly a word passed between the women as they walked the two miles into Dundalk. Disappointment was their reward when the policeman on duty would not allow Mary in to see her husband or his uncle. She tried begging, crying and berating but to no avail. Having settled herself down on the steps beside Maggie, she was nursing her baby when the head constable arrived and glared at them. Mary thought about approaching him but quickly changed her mind when she saw the scowl on his face.

"How long have those women been sitting out there?" he asked.

"That's James McGrother's wife and sister, sir. They've been taking it in turns all morning to come in and ask for permission to visit the prisoners. I told them we would have them for vagrancy if they didn't leave."

"Maybe we could use their visit to help us with our enquiries. I'm going to let the wife in to see her husband and I want you to listen to every word that passes between them. On no account are you to leave them unattended, understand?" the chief constable's scowl had turned into a cunning smile.

The young policeman nodded and went outside to fetch Mary.

"You are to be allowed in to visit with your husband for a short while. Your baby will have to remain outside. Follow me."

Mary jumped up, thrusting the infant into Maggie's arms. She grabbed the basket of food they had brought but the constable took it from her.

"There's no need to bring that in, they are most likely eating better than you," the young man said.

Having been warned not to approach James but remain seated on the opposite side of the table, Mary's heart raced at the thought of seeing him. She hoped she wouldn't cry, especially in front of the young constable, but as soon as her husband was brought into the room with his hands cuffed together, the tears spilled over.

"I'm sorry James, I didn't want to get upset in front of you," Mary looked at the policeman standing by the door. "Am I allowed to hold his hand?" she asked.

When the constable nodded and reminded them they must remain seated, James grabbed hold of his wife's hands so tight it made her wince.

"Mary, have you seen Uncle Pat? Is he still confused?"

"And I miss you too, James McGrother," Mary tried to lighten his mood.

"They won't let me talk to him. I don't know how he's faring. I'm worried to death over him, Mary."

"I'll see if they will let me visit him before I go, James. Have they told you why both of you are being kept here? Surely they don't suspect you of stealing anything, sure the teaspoon was found in Pat's clothing."

James replied that she knew as much as he did, "There has to be more to this. It wasn't the Crown jewels that was found in his jacket. All this fuss for a piece of cutlery, even if it was silver. You know how Pat has been lately, confused and forgetful, but he's not a thief," said James.

"I don't know what possessed him to take it but as soon as he realized what he had done, he would have returned it immediately, like he did with the bowls," said Mary.

James coughed and glanced quickly at the constable guarding them. He hadn't mentioned the bowls to the police during questioning, thinking it would make the situation worse.

Whether his uncle had spoken of the incident or not, James had no way of telling.

Their conversation was interrupted by two constables entering the room to take James away. Mary remained calm and blew a kiss as her husband was led through the door.

"Try and talk them into letting you see Pat. Make sure he's well, Mary. Kiss the children for me," James's words faded into the distance.

Mary was told to wait outside until sent for. She didn't ask to see Pat as her emotions were still reeling over the visit with James. Maggie listened as every word spoken between the young couple was repeated by Mary, until she was summoned to the chief constable's office.

"I have decided to let you visit your husband's uncle but I must warn you not to get him overly excited. He has been behaving himself all morning and I want him to stay that way. Do you understand, Mrs. McGrother, that it is in his best interest to remain calm and coherent?

"I do, sir, you have my word on it. I will do my very best to cheer him up with news about the children. He is like a grandfather to them and must be missing them sorely."

The head constable nodded and signalled to the young policeman standing by the door in the small room. As Mary was being led into the corridor she turned her face back towards the desk and thanked the man sitting behind it. He appeared to be stern and cold natured but she hoped there might be a sympathetic soul lying beneath the hard exterior.

Pat jumped up and ran to Mary as soon as she walked through the door. It took all of her inner strength to push him firmly away before the constable accompanying her could intervene.

"We must keep a distance between us, Uncle Pat, but we are allowed hold hands. Why don't we sit down?" Mary glanced at the policeman standing just inside the locked door.

Relieved at his nod of approval, she led the elderly man towards a rough wooden platform that served as a bed. Pat looked like he had aged ten years and appeared to be exhausted.

"James tells me the food here is very good indeed, Pat. I fear that when you get home my cooking will not be to your liking anymore," Mary gave a weak laugh.

"You have spoken to James? They will not let us see each other. Mary, they must think that James had a part in this. I have no recollection at all of taking that cursed teaspoon but I know for sure that James had nothing to do with it. I felt it in my jacket the moment I picked it up, but I was afraid to tell him about it on account of the incident with . . ."

"Now don't you get yourself all worked up again," Mary interrupted Pat before he said anything else that would add to the trouble he was already in.

"Mary, a stór. The next time you see James you must tell him that this will all be sorted out. I'm going to make everything right for him. Promise me that you will let him know and ease his mind. Will you do that for me?"

The old eyes that held Mary's gaze were clearer than she had seen them in a long time. Pat looked focused and sure of himself as he spoke. She nodded her head, lost for words.

Whatever he had decided to do had brought him to his senses and Mary did not want to say anything that might change that.

The young man on guard cleared his throat and informed Mary that her visiting time was up. He did not rush forward when she threw herself into Pat's arms to embrace him. The old fisherman patted her back, then pulled away to look her in the eye and made her promise once more to support him, no matter what she believed or how she felt.

CHAPTER ELEVEN

"Have those McGrother women decided to go back to their home yet?"

"They've just gone, sir. When I told them they could visit again tomorrow they were happy enough to pack up their belongings and leave," the young constable replied to his superior.

"Tell me again what was said about the bowls. You must write up your report immediately, while it is still fresh in your head."

"Well, sir, it was the woman who mentioned the bowls. She seemed to be under the impression that they were returned, but her husband quickly interrupted her and behaved in a very furtive manner at the mention of them. When Mrs. McGrother was visiting the old uncle she stopped him from speaking about a certain 'incident' he was involved in. He told her he had no recollection of taking the piece of cutlery and believed his nephew had nothing to do with it," the young constable felt very important relaying the information to his superior.

"Yes, well, you had better set to and get that report done. I must meet up with Lord Devereux and relay this latest piece of evidence to him. Surely they must have realized their pilfering would catch up with them? They look intelligent enough. It's possible the old man is innocent but delusional and that young nephew of his is taking advantage of his confusion," the head constable left the room shaking his head.

When Mary and Maggie arrived home there was a reception committee awaiting them. The neighbouring women had taken it upon themselves to find out as much information as they could about the goings on at Freemont House.

"It's no wonder your men have been sent to jail, someone's been pilfering the silverware. Young Alice O'Connor told her mother that the butler had the place pulled apart looking for two silver bowls missing from a set. Apparently there's supposed to be a dozen and they could only find ten," said one of the women.

"Alice says that the Master ordered a count of all the cutlery and it was discovered that there's several pieces missing from that too. They have so much silverware it wasn't noticed until recently," another woman added. "They are planning a ball and having everything cleaned and polished for the occasion."

"So they are blaming James and Pat," said Maggie, "I hope none of ye are thinking the same thing."

The women shook their heads and commiserated over such an unfortunate mistake. They agreed that Pat McGrother, even on one of his most confusing days, would never resort to such a thing. Mary thanked the women for their support and announced that she would be paying a visit to the O'Connors as soon as Alice returned home from her work at the big house.

Having assured the children that their father and Pat would be back with the family soon, Maggie sent them outside to play, then turned to her sister-in-law.

"Mary, I know by that look on your face that you are planning something. Be careful that you don't make the situation worse than it already is."

"I smell a rat and I'm going to find out who took that silverware. You know that everyone will blame Pat, on account of his mind being feeble at times. Even though the neighbours might tell us they believe he is innocent, between themselves they have him as guilty. Sure Pat himself told me that he is going to make it right. Even he thinks he might have been thieving while taking one of his turns. That old goat is going to take the blame and try to get James released," Mary placed a hand on Maggie's shoulder. "People won't talk to the police, you know that Maggie. If there's something needs telling, I've a much better chance of discovering it than any constable.

There was an awkward silence in the O'Connor house as Mary sipped her tea and tried to make small talk with Alice's parents. Michael O'Connor was one of the local fishermen and two of his sons worked alongside him on his boat. The boys excused themselves, giving their parents and Mary some privacy.

"I would be much obliged to you Alice, if you could tell me what you've heard about the missing silverware," Mary spoke softly to the girl.

Alice looked at her father, who nodded his head then stood up and announced he was leaving the women to talk among themselves. He patted Mary on the shoulder as he walked by, wishing her luck in getting her men released from prison and assuring her that nobody believed James was guilty of any crime.

"But you think Pat might be, do you Mr. O'Connor?" asked Mary.

"If Pat McGrother took something that did not belong to him, then I believe he did it while not in his senses. If that is the case, he will need to remember where the missing items are, or you will never be able to clear his name. I would wager the head constable is convinced that your husband has sold off that silver. If Pat took it he might be able to lead the police to where he has it hidden," Michael O'Connor put his cap on his head as he opened the door. "We will keep you all in our prayers, Mrs. McGrother."

Mary thanked the man before turning to his daughter, "Alice, I don't want you to tell me anything that might get you into trouble with your employers but if you've heard something you think might help my husband and his uncle, I would be very grateful if you would share it with me."

The young girl shifted uncomfortably on the hard bench she was seated upon. Her mother raised an eyebrow at her, a signal that she was waiting for her to speak.

"Come on now, girl, tell Mary exactly what you told us last night. I think it only fair that she should know what's being said up at the big house about her husband and his uncle."

"But Mammy, you have always told me not to repeat any gossip I hear when I'm at work. I don't want to lose my job over it."

"Please, Alice, I swear to you on Annie McGrother's grave that I won't tell a soul where I got my information from," Mary pleaded.

"I suppose anyone working at the big house could tell you this, Mrs. McGrother, so maybe there's no harm in it – as long as you forget it was me who told you," Alice waited until Mary nodded before going on. "Cook, Mrs. Lennon that is, had been looking for the dog's bowls everywhere and when the commotion started over the missing silverware there was a lot of jesting over the wooden bowls. We were all convinced the dog had run off with them and someone suggested following the animal to his secret hiding place and getting a reward for finding the missing silverware," Alice stopped when she saw Mary wince.

"I'm sorry, Alice, I'm not blaming you. It was the ridiculing of Annie's bowls that got to me. They were made by her uncle as a wedding present for her mother. You were not to know that, please go on."

"When the constables came to question us we were taken into the Master's study, one by one, and asked what we knew about the silverware. I told them the truth; that I knew nothing. I was very nervous. The only one who spoke was the head constable, while the other one took notes. The Master himself, never said a word and just sat at his desk listening and staring. If it was me who had taken the ware I would have surely confessed under the strain of it."

"So the silverware went missing before the wooden bowls, is that what you're saying, Alice?"

"Nobody rightly knows when it disappeared as it hadn't been used for a long time. The silver bowls were part of a set and it wasn't till they were about to be cleaned that anyone bothered to count them. Then all of the cutlery was gathered and some of that was missing too. The ructions it caused, remember Mammy? How you sent young Patrick to fetch me on account it was so late and no sign of me arriving home?"

"I was beside myself with the worry, Mary. I thought young Alice had met with an accident."

Mary smiled at the girl's mother and patted the back of her hand.

"Was it then that Mrs. Lennon mentioned the wooden bowls, Alice?"

"No, Mrs. McGrother. That was when the stable boy told her about seeing your husband's uncle with them. He said he didn't want to get the old man in trouble but now that something of value had gone missing he felt he should report it. We were all very nervous, you know how people are quick to point the finger and it's myself and the scullery maid who usually polish the silver. I was sure they would blame us and I'm sorry to say, I was much relieved that the attention was being put elsewhere."

"So Mrs. Lennon brought the stable boy to the Master to repeat his story, did she?" asked Mary.

"No, she went to Mr. Dixon, the butler, and told him. It was he that brought Peter up to the Master. I was there and saw it for myself, I thought he was going to have a fainting spell, he looked so pale and shook that much. Mr. Dixon had to steady him by holding onto his arm. We didn't see Peter until next morning, as we were all dismissed and allowed to go home while he was still in the study being questioned."

"Where does Peter live, Alice? I promise I won't breathe a word of this to anyone. I just want to talk to him, to ask him myself about the wooden bowls," asked Mary.

Alice looked to her mother for approval before revealing the boy's address. It was with a very heavy heart that Mary made her way back to the McGrother household. From what she had been told, the evidence was stacked so high against her husband's uncle that even she was beginning to doubt his innocence. The one thing Mary knew for sure, was that James himself had no part in any thieving that had been going on at the big house.

CHAPTER TWELVE

Constable Armstrong himself accompanied Mr. Harrington to the cell where James had been held for almost a week. The young solicitor had been approached by their priest and had agreed to take on their case, having first checked up on the men's reputation and character. As soon as they stepped through the door James stood to attention, as if he was a soldier in the presence of a commanding officer. It was an automatic reaction but the young fisherman immediately relaxed his stance, refusing to show respect to a man who had condemned him as guilty without the slightest bit of evidence.

"My name is William Harrington, I have taken on your case, Mr. McGrother, and you are to be released immediately," the young solicitor shook hands with James. "The police have no proof of your involvement in any crime that may have been committed," Harrington informed him.

"Does that apply to my uncle, too?"

Armstrong stepped forward, sneering, and pushed his face up close to his prisoner's. The two men were of equal height and James calmly held the stare that was meant to intimidate him.

"If it was up to me, McGrother, you would be on your way to Van Diemen's Land," snarled the constable, "To join your cousin. Francis wasn't it? Stole a cow from his landlord's herd. When was that? About a dozen years ago, I reckon. Thieving appears to run in your family, McGrother."

"His parents and neighbours were starving, he wasn't the only one involved," James could feel his temper rising. "But he took the blame alone, to save others from the same fate."

Mr. Harrington cleared his throat and took hold of James's arm, drawing him away from his antagonist. The young fisherman held the constable's vindictive stare and smiled at the words his solicitor used next.

"Fortunately, transportation is no longer a punishment, Constable Armstrong, and this man has not been convicted of any crime. He is free to go. James, come with me, I have already written out a report, ready for you to sign."

As they walked towards the doorway the constable slid his foot forward and James tripped over it.

"Watch your step, McGrother, because I'll be keeping my eye on you – and your family."

"Ignore him, James. He would give anything to arrest you for assaulting an officer of the Crown. I am sorely tempted to punch his sneering face myself," whispered Harrington.

While some sheets of paper were being placed in front of James, the head constable stood by the window, looking over the young man's shoulder. The solicitor pointed to where his client's signature was needed.

"Do you remember how to make your mark, McGrother? I can witness it, if you like," Constable Armstrong was enjoying making fun of someone he thought was illiterate.

James picked up a pen from its holder and dipped the nib into an ink bottle, then wrote his full name. Mr. Harrington took a wooden blotter and rolled it over the neat signature, smiling with satisfaction at the head constable.

"Mr. McGrother is well able to read and write, so there is no need to witness his mark. But you are required to witness his *signature*, are you not?"

The solicitor smiled at how well his words had deflated the arrogance of the man glaring at him from the other side of the desk. James found it difficult to keep his face straight as he held out the pen to the head constable, who snatched it from his hand.

"What about my uncle, Mr. Harrington? Where is he? Surely we are both free to go. Have they found the missing silverware?"

"James, please be patient. Let me take you for something to eat and we can discuss the situation. This is not the place."

Constable Armstrong's arrogance had returned and he shouted after James at the top of his voice, "Pat McGrother will be in jail for what is left of his dreary life, and you'll be joining him soon."

Mr. Harrington quickly steered his newly released prisoner out of the barracks and across the street towards an inn. He would not embarrass the young fisherman by taking him to the hotel where he usually dined, knowing he would be refused admittance dressed as he was.

"James, please eat something, you have lost weight this past week. Surely you do not want to alarm your wife when she sees you."

"Did my family know that I was to be released? And what about my uncle, why is he not with us?" James ate a dumpling from the bowl of stew, the aroma enticing him.

"I am still trying to obtain Pat's release, but I must warn you James, it does not bode well for him. Did you know he signed a confession?"

"Mr. Harrington, are you trying to tell me he will rot in jail over two wooden bowls?"

The solicitor shook his head while he tried to find an easy way to tell James exactly what the old fisherman had confessed to. "No James, not just Annie's bowls. Pat says he believes he must have taken the silverware while in a confused state of mind."

James jumped up from the table, causing an immediate lull in the hum of conversation surrounding them. Mr. Harrington remained sitting but tugged at the young man's jacket, urging him to take his seat.

"James, I warned your uncle that under no circumstances was he to admit to anything. He obviously didn't listen. The poor man seems to think it was in your best interest for him to confess to a crime that I am almost certain he did not commit," the solicitor said.

"Poor old fool, does he really think he is a thief? Anybody will tell you that there isn't a more honest man than Pat McGrother," James lowered himself back onto his stool, running a hand through his hair.

"I'm sorry to bring this up now, but was your uncle not part of a group of men caught poaching on the Freemont estate some years ago. The only reason I mention this is because it will be used in court against him," Harrington's voice was full of sympathy.

The young fisherman stared open-mouthed at the man sitting opposite him, "That was at a time when the whole country was starving.

Surely it will not be held against him. There had been no boats put out to sea for over a week, on account of the weather. Some of the older men took it upon themselves to get food for the village by bringing a boat up the Fane and they managed to land enough to feed their families for another few days. They were caught by the game warden but the landlord let them off with a warning, being aware of their troubles at the time. Where did you come by that story? Have the police been told about it?"

"I'm sorry, James. Yes, the head constable is aware of that particular event and the fact that you were not involved is the only reason you are not in jail right now. Lord Devereux mentioned it to the police during the investigation."

"Pat never told me of his plans to go up the river. The only ones who knew of it were the four men who went. They agreed amongst themselves that no young man, nor anyone with a family to support, should take the risk. Pat went because I was there to take care of Annie, should he be caught. I cannot believe they will bring that up, all these years later," said James.

"The police are building a case against him, even though your uncle has confessed. They mean to show a history of theft in order to make a more solid conviction. They want to be sure the judge will sentence Pat to the maximum number of years allowed. Do you see how precarious his situation is, James?"

"I do, Mr. Harrington, and I'm very grateful to you for getting me out of jail, but you must now do everything in your power to have my uncle released, too. I fear he will not last much longer if left in there. Surely he is entitled to spend whatever years God has left for him in the company of his family? Even if he did take the silverware in his confusion, we will watch him every minute of the day and search high and low for it, until it is found. Would that satisfy the judge, Mr. Harrington?"

The solicitor gave a sad smile and shook his head, "It would not be as simple as that, James. Your wife came to me with some information but I am not at liberty to discuss it yet, and not here of all places. She will tell you herself when you arrive home. Your uncle has done you no favours in making a confession. Constable Armstrong is convinced that as fast as Pat was taking the silverware, confused or not, you were selling it. I want your word that you will not do anything foolish while your uncle awaits trial. Do I have it, Mr. McGrother?"

James gave his word and asked if he was free to go. The only place he wanted to be at that moment was with his family. Mr. Harrington offered to arrange some transport but James declined, saying he would prefer to walk and would feel better for the exercise. The two men shook hands as they parted company. As the solicitor sat back down to finish his meal he noted that James had hardly touched his food. He sincerely hoped the McGrother family would be prepared for the harsh verdict he feared would be the outcome of the case.

CHAPTER THIRTEEN

"Was it very bad, James? Maggie says I should get you to talk to me. She says it does a body no good to keep things locked inside. She says . . ."

"She says, she says, she says. Maggie doesn't know everything. There are some things not meant to be shared," James felt his wife's body stiffen beside him. "I'm sorry, Mary, I didn't mean any disrespect. My sister has an uncanny way of reading a man's thoughts and it can be very unsettling. That was why I avoided answering her questions when I arrived home today."

Mary relaxed once more in the circle of her husband's arms. "Mr. Harrington sent a message yesterday informing us that he was certain you would be released today. We have all been on edge waiting for your return, afraid that something would happen to change their minds," Mary settled her head more comfortably on James's shoulder. "Maggie sat on the wall staring up the road for hours before she saw you. I watched the wee ones join her for a while, then run off to play, but she never left the wall. She feels more like a mother to you than a sister, James. You cannot blame her for being concerned. Besides, I believe what she says is true – about holding bad feelings inside of us."

James sighed deeply. He had been waiting for Mary to share her own news with him and believed that was what she would do, once they were alone. Instead, she was asking him questions that only served to make him more anxious.

"Fine so, I will tell you what it was like in jail. The food was palatable, the bed hard, the neighbours noisy and I did not have to suffer cold feet pressed against my calves when I lay down at night," whispered James. "Does that satisfy your curiosity?"

Mary dug her knuckles into his ribs and laughed, "As pleasant as your stay was, I hope you are not given another opportunity to partake of Her Majesty's hospitality."

Maggie was upstairs, sleeping with the children and the quietness of the house was broken only when a wave could be heard crashing on the beach nearby.

"Don't you have something to tell me yourself, Mary? Mr. Harrington seems to think you do."

"I do, James, but you won't like it. One of the stable boys swore an oath that he saw Pat placing Annie's bowls in the long grass by one of the walls you repaired."

"What harm can that do? A pair of old bowls they thought fit only for a dog. They cannot keep an old man in jail for such a paltry offense. We can pay whatever fine the judge sets, there is no need . . ."

"*James*, listen to me. Annie's bowls are not the problem – besides, they have been returned. Two silver bowls have gone missing from a set. They were a wedding present to Lord and Lady Devereux from the Marquess of Bath. There are pieces of cutlery missing too, some fish knives and teaspoons. It seems that Pat must have been taking whatever he could fit in his pocket whenever the urge came over him."

"Mary, are you listening to yourself? How can you think such a thing? Has even one piece of that missing silverware been found here and if not, what do you suppose Uncle Pat has done with it all?" James's voice was getting louder as he spat out the words.

"Hush, you will have the whole house awake. Have you forgotten the spoon that was found in his jacket? The police think that Pat meant to bury it until it could be sold. They also believe that you, James, had a part in the selling of the cursed objects. Mr. Harrington says they have no evidence to prove anything of the sort but he fears that the head constable bears a grudge against you. He says we must be careful not to draw any attention upon ourselves. He's a good man, James, and I trust him to do his best for Pat."

"I cannot for the life of me believe that Pat McGrother took anything other than those two wooden bowls, but tomorrow we are going to search high and low. If there is anything to be found then find it we must. I saw that your flowers have all been tampered with in the garden, Mary. Was that the handiwork of the police?"

"It was, but the children did their best to replant them. Let's go to sleep now, James, we can talk more in the morning. Mr. Harrington might even have some good news for us."

After an early breakfast, Mary sent the children off to school. Maggie excused herself by saying she would accompany them, feeling the need to stretch her legs, which made James laugh. His sister had never liked long walks, even as a child.

"How thoughtful of Maggie to leave us with the house to ourselves," James came up behind Mary as she was sweeping a pile of dust through the doorway. He slid his arms around her waist, kissing the side of her neck.

"James McGrother, are you planning on doing any work at all today? Have you not got some fishing to do, or is your stomach still full on Her Majesty's fancy food?"

"Oh woman, you have a sharp tongue on you this morning. I told you last night that I am going to search for that silverware Pat is supposed to have stolen," James lifted a shovel from where it rested against the side of the dresser and headed towards the open door.

Mary ran after him in a panic, calling his name. She did not want James to go around to the back of the cottage but he strode ahead, ignoring her pleas. Turning the corner of the house, she bumped into her husband, who was standing very still surveying what was left of the garden his aunt had spent most of her life cultivating. Mature fruit bushes lay wilted having been pulled from the ground, while huge holes were to be seen dotted randomly here and there.

"The police had no right to cause so much damage. There was no need to uproot everything in sight," James's voice broke as he sank to his knees on the damp, upturned sods.

"I tried to tell them that if they spared the roots by digging deep enough then the plants would survive, but they wouldn't listen. Maggie was shouting and pulling at their arms until one of the constables pushed her away and she fell to the ground. It was a blessing the children where all at school. We managed to save a few of the younger bushes, look, James," Mary was jumping over the holes, moving from one wilted plant to another. "See, this one seems a little fresher than it was yesterday. And that one over there is much livelier, too."

James picked himself up without uttering a word and raised the shovel high above his head before stabbing it into the loose clay. Turning abruptly on his heel, the young man stormed away from his home, heading for Paddy Mac's. Although he had never been prone to drinking, it was the one thing he felt most in need of at that moment, to quell the rage building up inside him.

After a few attempts at repairing the damaged shrubbery, Mary gave up and turned towards the cottage, shaking her head in frustration. Her sister-in-law was leaning against the gable wall with her arms folded across her chest.

"I was wondering when you would notice my presence. I've been standing here listening to you ranting and raving like a mad woman. James marched past me on the road with a face like thunder. Did you two have a disagreement over the landscaping?" Maggie, as usual, tried to make light of the situation.

Mary shot her a scathing look and sliced the shovel into the earth, much as James had done but with a lot less force, then strode past her. When she entered the house, Mary gasped with dismay to see an old scratched tea caddy lying on its side on the dresser, the lid gaping open like a hungry mouth. Maggie ran forward and picked it up, shaking it, as if by some miracle the rent money would still be in there, clinging to the bottom.

"We both know where he's going and it will do no good to try and stop him," said Mary.

"What has gotten James so riled? He never paid much heed to the garden before."

"Oh Maggie. I as much as told him last night that I believed while Pat's mind was addled, he had taken the missing silverware. It near broke his heart to hear me say it. I never mentioned the fact that the police had dug up the back garden. I knew it would keep him awake all night, thinking about it. Before I got a chance to tell him this morning, he grabbed the shovel with the intention of searching the garden himself for the silverware. More to prove me wrong than to find it, I reckon," Mary sat down heavily on her husband's chair, by the fireside.

The only other chair in the room was the one Pat always sat on and Maggie eased herself onto its woven rush seat. For a long time, the two women stared silently into the white ash, left over from a turf fire the night before. The hens came clucking into the cottage one by one, picking at the ground until Mary shooed them through the door.

"Do you think I should call to Paddy Mac's and see how James is faring?"

"You might make things worse if you do that, Mary. No man wants his wife leading him home by the ear," said Maggie. "Paddy Mac will make sure he gets back safe and sound. I doubt that anyone besides James will be drinking at this hour of the day."

As the time dragged by, the two women busied themselves preparing food for when the children arrived home from school. A portion was set aside for Pat, who loved a bit of salted herring, and Mary was planning on bringing it to him the next day on her visit. A knock on the open door made both women jump. They turned around to see Kitty Carroll, the woman who had delivered all of the McGrother children, standing in the doorway.

"Bless us and save us, you two are a bag of nerves, aren't ye?" Kitty sat on one of the chairs warming her hands over the fire. "Are ye missing a man, by any chance?" she asked.

"We know exactly where he is, Kitty, and what condition he is likely to be in by now. My James never could hold his drink," said Mary.

"And aren't you the fortunate woman for that? He's likely to pass out before all your rent money is gone then, isn't he?" laughed Kitty.

"Have you just come from Paddy Mac's? Surely he has not taken every penny from James?" asked Maggie as she placed a cup of tea into their visitor's hands.

"Paddy is a good man, he would never take advantage of anyone. As I was passing by his open door I heard raised voices inside and sure curiosity got the better of me. Mary, that poor man of yours is hurting bad. I've never seen James McGrother with that much drink on him. Paddy signalled for me to come in and we tried to reason with him. He kept throwing what was left of his money at Paddy and cursing him for not serving him. In the end I saw him pour a huge glass of whiskey for James and place the money back into his pocket, unbeknownst to him."

"Has he passed out so?" asked Maggie.

"I would say he is near enough to doing that by now," replied Kitty. "Paddy asked me to fetch Joseph White on my way here. He says that between the two of them, they will get James to sleep it off in Joseph's house. James would be very upset when he sobers up if he was to learn that his wee ones had seen him in such a state."

"Well I thank ye all for your kindness and for sparing his pride, not that he deserves it," said Mary.

"Ah now, give the man a chance, woman. He's entitled to let off some steam once in a while," scolded Maggie. "We will leave it up to James to come home when he's ready. Would you be so kind as to inform Joseph White of that, Kitty, so he can relay the message to my brother when he recovers from his – em – unfortunate malady."

Kitty promised she would and thanked the women for the tea. Patting Mary on the back before walking towards the doorway, she told her there was many a woman would give their right arm for a man like James McGrother, drink and all.

CHAPTER FOURTEEN

James groaned as he lifted his pain filled head. A beam of sunlight shining through a small window above made him feel worse, so he lay back down and closed his eyes. He tried to remain in that position as it caused him less pain but his stomach had other ideas. As the bile began to rise, James shot up and ran for the door.

The sound of heaving outside gave Joseph White a sick feeling in his own stomach, even though he had not indulged in too much drink himself the day before. He centred a black kettle on top of the banked fire, the weight of it waking up the glowing embers. "I have some water on the boil, James, a cup of tea will settle your stomach," Joseph said to a very unsteady man coming through the doorway.

"I'm very grateful to you, Joseph, for bringing me to your house instead of my own. I would not have liked my family to see me in such a state. Did I do anything yesterday I might regret?" asked James.

"Are you not regretting the way you feel this morning?" laughed Joseph. "You did give Paddy Mac an awful tongue lashing for refusing to give you any more drink, but he just laughed at you and told me to take you away to my place. That was in the afternoon and you've been asleep since then. Don't worry about Mary. Kitty Carroll told her you would be staying with me. Still, I wouldn't like to be in your shoes when you face your wife – or your sister."

James's hand had shot to his pocket at the mention of Paddy Mac and he groaned at the empty space inside it. Joseph reached into his own pocket and withdrew some coins, placing them on an upturned wooden crate that served as a seat. With only two young fishermen living in the house, it was very sparsely furnished. A lot of poorer homes at that time did not have a table but ate around the fireplace.

"Paddy Mac told me to make sure you brought these coins back to your wife on your return home. You kept flinging them at him even though he refused to take them."

"He's a good man. And you are too, Joseph, thank you. They might help to cool Mary's temper a wee bit."

The hot tea helped to settle James's stomach but he shook his head at the potato that was offered to him. It was left over from the day before but was still warm, having been stored in a pot by the fire.

"I don't think I will risk anything solid, Joseph, if you don't mind. Is your brother out in the boat? Don't tell me you have missed a night's fishing because of me."

"Ah, James, do you think I would do that? You didn't need me to mind you while you slept. Patrick is staying over in Ardee for a few days, doing some labouring. There were no boats out last night, do you not remember what the weather was like?" asked Joseph.

"I wasn't paying any heed to it, I was so riled up about my uncle. Did you know the police destroyed Annie's garden? It will kill him to see it like that when he comes home," James bent down to pick his cap up from where it had landed on the floor the night before, and winced with the stab of pain that shot through his head. "I think I'm ready to face Mary now. It was very kind of you to look after me, Joseph. I'm in your debt."

The young man shook the hand that was held out to him and assured James that there would no doubt come a time when he might need the same favour himself, "Sure isn't that what neighbours do, watch out for each other," Joseph remarked.

It was a very sheepish James that poked his head through the doorway of the McGrother house. His wife and sister were silently preparing food at the large table that stood in the centre of the cottage. Mary caught sight of him out of the corner of her eye but pretended not to notice. Maggie carried on kneading dough into a round of bread ready for baking over the fire. She, too, was aware of James hovering just outside the door.

"Ahem," James was tempted to run as soon as he uttered the sound.

"Well? What are you waiting for? Permission to enter your own home?" asked Mary, without looking up from her work.

Maggie placed the dough into a large black cauldron and put a lid on top, before lowering it into the midst of the fire. "I have a few errands to run, Mary. I daresay the children will be finished school by the time I'm done," she brushed past her brother, digging him lightly in the ribs. "And you, James McGrother, have something to say to your wife, I imagine."

Mary never lifted her head nor uttered a word as her sister-in-law left the cottage. She carried on kneading her own batch of bread, even though it was ready for baking. Unable to keep her hands still, Mary took her frustration out on the soft dough, lifting it high before slamming it back onto the table, over and over. The sound of the tea caddy lid being opened reached her ears, and the noise of coins hitting the bottom told her that James had not spent all of their money.

Mary spun around, "Oh James. I was afraid we would not be able to pay the rent. I am truly sorry for doubting you."

"Paddy Mac refused to take all my money. He's a good man, Mary, but there is hardly enough left to pay for a month's rent, never mind two. It's me who should be apologizing to you, love," James stood with his back to his wife, too ashamed to face her.

Three short steps brought Mary close enough to wrap her arms around him. She pressed herself into his back, leaning her head against him, and squeezed as tight as she could. There was no need for words. Whenever conflict or disagreement came between them, all it ever took to bring them back together, was for one to make that gesture of reassurance to the other.

James spun around and scooped Mary up in one swift movement, no longer aware of his uneasy stomach. She smiled and wrapped her arms around his neck, before throwing a quick glance across the room at their sleeping baby.

CHAPTER FIFTEEN

The fishing had not been good and the portion of the catch that James held onto for himself was not enough to cover the shortfall for the following month's rent. Mary took what little there was and set off for the early morning market in Dundalk. James pretended to walk home and waited until his wife had turned the bend in the road before doubling back and getting into his boat once more. Joseph White had agreed to help him row across the bay to Carlingford, where a group of men would be waiting for his arrival.

The two men rowed without speaking for a long time until James broke the silence.

"It was a blessing meeting that Robinson man at Mr. Harrington's office this week. The money from this boat will feed my family and pay the rent until I have earned enough in England to send home," said James.

"There'll be more than enough. Surely you could have held onto your boat if you plan on going to England. You know the landlord would have waited for your rent, he has obliged his tenants before."

"I need the money now, Joseph, for my uncle. Money talks, you know that yourself, and the more you have the louder it speaks. I was meant to overhear that conversation between Robinson and Mr. Harrington, about him looking for a boat. I'm telling you, it was fate."

"We are only halfway there. Are you sure you want to do this?" asked Joseph, easing up on the oars.

"It's not a case of what I want," James replied sharply and changed the subject. "We could do with a bit of wind behind us, this boat needs at least three men to get anywhere fast."

Joseph knew by his tone of voice that James did not want to speak about the task ahead, so he concentrated on his rowing, matching that of his friend's. It wasn't too long before the ruin of King John's castle towering over Carlingford lough came into view. As they drew close to the pier a group of men waved at James and Joseph. The boat and its sail and tackle were closely examined, and after a lot of haggling a price was agreed upon. The two men who had purchased the boat between them offered to bring him as far as Dundalk in the vessel, but James declined, using an excuse about having some business in Carlingford to attend to. He couldn't bear to get back into the boat knowing it was no longer his.

"If you don't mind bringing me part of the way, I would be very grateful. I'm sure my friend can find his own way home," said Joseph.

Having walked for half an hour, James accepted a seat on a cart that had pulled up alongside him. The elderly driver talked about everything from religion to politics for the entire journey. At times, James wondered if he might walk faster than the ass that was pulling them, but he was glad of the opportunity to think about the sorry task that lay ahead. The words of the old man next to him blended with the rhythmic sound of hooves as James became lost in his own thoughts.

When the cart finally stopped it was beside a store, near the centre of Dundalk, and James expressed his appreciation for the lift by leaving a coin in the old man's hand as he shook it. It was only a ten minute walk to the prison where Pat McGrother had been held for the past three weeks. James's feet became heavier with every step that brought him nearer to his uncle.

"The head constable is away for the day so I will let you in to see him," the policeman on duty told James. "You are aware of his failing health, are you not?"

"I'm not blind, I can see it every time I am allowed to visit with him. Is there no mercy to be had for a sick old man?"

"Look, McGrother, do not take that tone with me. Personally, I find it hard to believe that you and your uncle would have enough intelligence between you to organize a large scale theft, the likes of which Constable Armstrong has stumbled upon. That is the only reason why I am allowing you this visit."

James was not offended by the insult, he was far more upset by the remark made about his uncle's health.

"Please excuse my bad manners, there was no call for me to speak like that to an officer of the Crown," the young fisherman would have gotten down on his knees and begged for forgiveness if it was the only way of seeing his uncle.

"There's no need to grovel, McGrother. Just don't mention this visit to the head constable, or he'll have my guts for garters," replied the policeman, as he led James to the holding cells at the back of the building. "I'm afraid I cannot unlock the door. I have strict instructions that no visitors be allowed enter the prisoner's cell, unless authorized by Constable Armstrong himself. As it is, I should never have brought you back here. You have five minutes and I will be waiting right over there," he pointed to an area further along the corridor.

"Thank you, I'm much obliged," James looked in through a tiny barred window in the centre of the thick wooden door.

As his eyes adjusted to the dim light, a heap of crumpled clothing in a dark corner opposite the door told James that his uncle was unaware of his visit. He called his name out three times before any movement could be seen and the face that looked up in response, chilled him to the bone.

"Uncle Pat, it's me, James, your nephew. Can you come nearer, I have good news for you?"

The old man coughed and wheezed as he pulled himself into a standing position, pausing to lean against the cold stone wall. As he shuffled unsteadily towards the door, James became aware of the stench of body odour, and more. He poked his index finger through the bars and pointed to an upturned metal chamber pot on the floor next to the low wooden bed.

"Have you knocked over your pot?" asked James.

Pat looked in the direction being pointed out to him then turned to his nephew. The look of confusion on his face caused James to change the subject. He didn't want to sacrifice any more of the precious minutes that were slipping by. The stains and smells attached to the old man's clothing gave him the answer to his question.

Turning to speak to the waiting constable, James enquired about the last time his uncle had access to soap and clean water to wash himself.

"Prisoners are permitted to wash once a week, but he has refused to do so. He is only in a holding cell, in prison he would be forced to wash. I daresay we may have to do the same if the smell gets any worse."

"James, have you come to fetch me home son?" Pat grabbed hold of his nephew's fingers that were still poking through the bars.

The young man struggled to swallow a lump that had formed in his throat.

"Not today, Uncle Pat, but I promise I will have you out of here soon. I have the money to do that now and I'll be paying a visit to Mr. Harrington as soon as I leave you. You will be back home in your own bed before you know it."

"What money? Why do you need money? Are ye behind in the rent?" Pat was getting anxious.

"No, not at all. We have more than enough for the rent. I got an advance on some walls that need repairing," James was thinking fast, surprised at how lucid his uncle was at that moment.

"James, you have never lied to me, have you?" the old man paused, waiting for an answer. His face was pressed up close to the bars, his blue eyes clear and piercing.

"No, I have always been honest with you, even when I knew it would get me into trouble," James could not tear his eyes away from his uncle's face and his mouth went dry as he prepared himself for what was coming.

"You promised me you would wait for a year before making any decision about your boat," sighed Pat. "*That* is where the money came from. Can you tell me I'm wrong, James?"

"I don't care about the boat. As soon as we get you home I'll be on my way to England. I can always get another one in a year or two," they both knew that was unlikely.

The old fisherman squeezed his nephew's hands and James had to hold his breath at the sickening smell of body waste drifting through the opening in the door. Both men had their fingers curled around the bars and James could not hold back the hot tears that stung his eyes. The look of disappointment on the face of someone who had been a father to him for the past ten years was too much to bear.

"I'm sorry. I'm truly sorry. Do you want me to try and buy it back? He seems decent enough, the man that bought my boat, he might return it if I explain how much it means to us," James sniffed, wiping his nose across the cuff of his jacket, still holding onto the bars. He did not want to break the contact with the old, calloused fingers curled around his own.

Pat shook his head slowly as he withdrew his hands and turned to walk away. James heard him call out to Annie and knew that, once again, he had lost the old fisherman to whatever memory had taken over his senses at that moment.

Repeatedly calling out to his uncle made no difference and Pat continued to sit in the same corner James had found him in, muttering to himself. The policeman standing a little distance away, more to avoid the smell than to give the men privacy, cleared his throat. When

James turned around he gestured that the time was up.

One last glance was enough to tell the young fisherman that his uncle was happier left to his memories. James felt it would be wrong to try and bring him back to the present, where he was a prisoner, separated from his family and disappointed with his nephew. He whispered through the bars that he would be back next day with good news. It was said more to console himself than his uncle, who was smiling and nodding his head as if deep in conversation with someone sitting beside him.

William Harrington drained the last few drops of tea from his china cup as he watched James McGrother cross the street below. He could tell how wretched the young man felt by the slump of his shoulders and the way he dragged his feet. Harrington sighed as he placed the cup back on its saucer. His father had warned him not to get personally involved in cases where there was no money to be earned, so he had been careful to choose only a few each year that he considered genuine. The McGrother case was one of them.

The sound of his clerk's raised voice coming from the outer room snapped Harrington out of his thoughts. He opened his door to the sight of James McGrother wringing his cap in his hands, asking to have a quick word. "James, come in, come in. Have you news of your uncle?" the solicitor said, nodding to the clerk.

Pulling a chair out from a large mahogany desk for his client to sit on, Harrington offered to have a fresh pot of tea made.

"No thank you, Mr. Harrington. I won't take up too much of your time. I just came to pay you for the work you have done on my behalf – and for what you are doing for my uncle. You are a good man, my family is much obliged to you."

"Mr. McGrother, there is no need to give me any payment. Besides, your uncle is still a prisoner and you are not quite out of the water yourself, yet. I thought I made that clear the last time we spoke."

James stood up and walked towards the window to survey the busy street two floors below. Saint Patrick's Church, unfinished in spite of being built a decade before, stood opposite, majestically cathedral-like. Its completion had been interrupted by the same hungry, desperate years that had failed to drive James and Mary from their beloved land.

"Can I not offer to pay for the loss of the silverware?" James watched as an elderly gentleman helped his wife across the street, halting a carriage in the process.

"Even if you had the money, the case cannot be heard in petty sessions as it is a serious crime of grand larceny. As Lord Devereux is the complainant, he cannot act as magistrate. The case has been assigned to the quarterly sessions and your uncle must remain in custody until the trial."

James spun around, "But that is months from now, Pat will never last till then. I have money. I sold my boat – here," he produced a cloth bag from his pocket and emptied notes and coins onto the polished desktop.

William Harrington looked sadly at an amount of money that would barely cover the cost of his own expenses, were he to charge them.

"I'm sorry James, that won't change anything. It may be useful for the payment of a fine, so keep it safe until then."

He gathered the money scattered across his desk and placed it back into the bag, before handing it to James.

"It is difficult enough keeping *you* out of jail. Constable Armstrong is fully convinced of your guilt and is doing his best to build a case against you. I hope you have a bill of sale for your boat."

"I do, Mr. Harrington," James took the paper from his pocket and held it out.

"Good man. I will keep this safe for you, if you don't mind. Would you like me to hold onto the money too?"

James thought for a moment, then tipped the bag upside down emptying some coins onto his palm and placing them in his pocket. "I'll just take enough for two month's rent and a bit to spare. I appreciate your concern Mr. Harrington and your kindness."

The solicitor counted what was left in the bag and wrote a note recording the amount of money he would be holding for James. As he handed it to him, he assured the young man of his confidence that his uncle's trial would have a favourable result. The solicitor hoped he had sounded much more positive than he felt.

CHAPTER SIXTEEN

Having no appetite for the breakfast placed in front of him, James stared at the coins sitting in a neat, freshly counted pile on the table. Mary had taken the news about the boat better than he had expected, which helped ease some of the guilt he was feeling. He had put the money on the table as soon as Maggie left to walk the children to school. She had taken to a ramble each morning, paying a visit to one house in particular on her return home.

"I think your sister has a fancy man, James. You need to have a word with her, she has been very secretive lately."

"And what business would that be of mine, she has a mind of her own and I'm merely the wee brother."

"You are the man of the house, James McGrother, and quite capable of making decisions on your own – even foolish ones like this," Mary pointed to the money on the table, "You had better not tell Pat about the boat, it would break his heart."

"He knows already. I didn't have to tell him, when I said I had some money that would help get him out of jail, he guessed where it had come from. It was never my intention to speak about it but he was in such a desperate state, I wanted to give him some hope," James sat opposite his wife, elbows resting on the table, his palms covering his face.

Reaching across, Mary took hold of her husband's wrists and drew his hands away from his face. Her heart ached for him when she saw how tormented he was.

"I broke a promise I made to him, Mary. I told him I would not even think about selling the boat for a year, then I went behind his back without even consulting him on it. He will never forgive me."

"Don't feel so bad, my love, your intentions were good and Pat will realize that in time. Sure he's forgiven you already, I know he has. I prayed this morning that we will be allowed in to visit with him today. God is good, you'll see, James, and we will all feel better by this evening."

"I can't face him just yet, Mary. You and Maggie go yourselves. Bring him the food you've put by for him. That will cheer him up."

James smiled weakly but his wife knew his heart would remain sad and heavy for a long time. She had betrayed the trust of the elderly fisherman herself, not too long before, and the guilt was still hanging over her.

"I, too, broke a promise I had made to Pat. I told him I would not go against anything he said or did, no matter how I felt or what I believed. He doesn't know that I spoke to Mr. Harrington about him and I will be called as a witness in his defence. We decided it was best not to say too much about it to Pat, his mind being of a fragile nature and all," Mary sighed and walked around the table to rest her hands on James's shoulders. "So you see, my love, you are not the only one to have broken a promise to him. I dread to see his face when he finds out that I have done the same."

At that moment Maggie burst through the doorway with the children, her face red from running. She glared at her younger brother when she saw the money lying on the table, "So it is true," she said, taking a seat by the fire. "You sold the boat."

"No you didn't, Daddy, tell her she's wrong. The men took it out this morning without you, isn't that so?" cried Catherine.

"You should have taken the children to school first, Maggie, before coming back here to berate your brother," Mary was annoyed at the intrusion.

Thomas stood beside James, placing a hand on his father's shoulder. He knew as soon as he saw the money the story about the boat was true. The young boy believed there would be a good reason for selling it, compassion and solidarity for his father sweeping away his disappointment. "We will get another boat, Daddy. I can find work, you'll see."

James patted his son's hand before reaching across the table to gather up the money. Putting it into the bag and drawing the string tight, he held it out to his wife.

"Put this in a safe place, Mary, where I cannot find it – I don't trust myself anymore. I am going to ask for work on the Freemont estate, I heard they had a fallen tree topple a wall this week. On the way back I'll pay a visit to Paddy Mac's. No better place to put the word around that I'm looking to join a crew.

"What in heaven's name possessed you to get rid of your boat, James? We could have arranged a loan for the rent. Where you drunk when you sold it?"

"Leave him be, Maggie. He did it for Pat, not for the rent. Mr. Harrington has most of it in his office and says he won't touch a penny for himself but it may be of use in some other way," Mary said in defence of her husband.

"Does Pat know about this?" asked Maggie.

James nodded, "I had no intention of telling him when I was allowed a five minute visit yesterday, but he looked so pathetic. I wanted to give him something to hold onto while he awaits his trial. Did you know that it must go to the quarterly sessions?"

Both women were shocked at the news. Mary took hold of Mary-Ann's hand and pulled Thomas away from his father. She needed to get out from under the misery that hung in the air of her house.

"Come along, children. There is no need for ye to miss a whole day of schooling. I'll walk ye back up the road," she ignored their complaining and turned around before stepping through the doorway. "I think you have a matter you need to discuss with your sister, James, and it's not something that these little ears should be listening to, is it?"

When they were alone Maggie stood in front of James with her hands on her hips, "Well, what have you got to say for yourself? Although there is nothing can convince me you were right to sell that boat."

"She wasn't talking about the boat, Maggie. I don't quite know how to put this to you. I am the man of this house and as your brother, whether youngest or not, I have the right to ask this of you. Have you been keeping company with a man without telling us?" James sighed.

"Is that what Mary says? Could she not have asked me to my face, instead of gossiping behind my back to my wee brother?"

"Will you stop calling me that, I'm a good six inches taller than you," James stood up to prove his point. "Her exact words were that you had a 'fancy man' and I'm inclined to believe her, judging by your reaction."

Maggie could not stay mad at her brother for long. The look on his face as he tried to exercise some authority over her, made her laugh almost as much as the idea of them thinking she had a secret admirer. She knew that the real reason for her regular visits to the cottage of Michael and Sean McGuinness could never be revealed and had an answer already prepared for such a question. Gossip was quick to spread in small communities and stories became embellished as they were passed along.

"I have been mending their clothes, sure the poor old souls have no woman to look after them since their sister passed away. I made some bread for them too, you should have tasted the results of their attempts. How they are not poisoned I'll never know. Does that ease your mind now, James?"

The young man breathed a sigh of relief, "Can't you bring the clothes here to mend. It would look better, Maggie."

"Sure I've finished with them now. It's not as if they have a trunk full of trousers, is it? But I fully intend on keeping up my visits and baking them a batch of bread when I do. They are lost for a bit of female company and it takes my mind off my own troubles to help them. Now what have you got to say about that, *wee brother?*" asked Maggie, her temper rising.

James knew better than to push his sister any further on the subject. He had far more important things on his mind, like finding some work. The money he had held onto from the sale of his boat would helped cover a couple of month's rent, but it wouldn't last long if he was to continue dipping into it. James put on his cap as he walked towards the door.

"Right. Well, I've done my duty as the man of the house. Wouldn't you agree, Maggie?"

"I would, James. There's no one can fault you there. Now, you go on about *your* business and I'll get on with *mine*," Maggie held out some warm potatoes she had taken from a pot over the fire. "Take these with you. With any luck you'll find a bit of work for the day and you'll need to keep your strength up for it."

As James was leaving the house he saw Mary approach. It was too late for him to turn and head the other way so he braced himself. Passing him by, she slowed down to whisper, "Did you have a word with Maggie?"

James nodded sternly and carried on walking, relieved that he had left the house before his wife's return. He knew that Maggie would pretend to be in agreement with them, but still carry on as she herself saw fit.

When Mary bustled through the doorway, prepared for a confrontation, Maggie greeted her in a friendly manner. "You look the better for your walk. I have some tea brewed, do you want a cut of bread to go along with it?" she asked.

Mary studied her sister-in-law's face for any sign of resentment but all she saw was a warm smile. "Thank you kindly, Maggie. I was thinking of bringing the children with me to see Pat. Do you think we could sneak around the back and lift them up to the window?"

"Do you want to frighten the life out of them? From what James has told us they would hardly recognize the poor man, and he may very well be confused as to who is peering in through the bars at him. No, Mary, I think it would be a mistake to do that, but they are your wee ones and you must do whatever you feel is best."

The words were spoken in a friendly manner but Mary knew they had a deeper meaning and realized that no matter what James had said to his sister, she was her own woman. A deep sigh and a sip of tea gave Mary some time to gather her thoughts.

"I suppose you are right, Maggie. We must all make up our own minds and suffer whatever the consequences may be," she took a bite from her bread. "I think what you said about confusing Pat may be true. It would be unfair to make him any worse than he is."

CHAPTER SEVENTEEN

Walking past his children's school, James reflected on his own childhood, on the hopes and dreams he had shared with his brothers growing up. The building, which earlier that day had rung with the voices of students chanting their lessons, was empty and silent. The evening was drawing in and he had been walking and thinking most of the day.

James grew more and more anxious when he received the same answer to every enquiry he made about work – there was nothing available. Normally he would be given the name of someone who might be able to put a day's work his way. The strained conversation at each call he made, was a clear indication of how difficult it would be for James to find any kind of work. He never for one moment thought that his brief time spent in custody and his uncle's imprisonment would have such a serious impact on his ability to earn a living.

As James approached Paddy Mac's the sound of men's laughter drifted towards him and a lantern, burning in the window, beckoned him into the warmth and companionship he was in need of at that moment. The offer of a place on a crew was made to the young fisherman as Paddy Mac put a mug of porter in front of him. "On the house, James," he said. "On account of your troubles."

James put a coin on the table, "I can pay for my drink Paddy, for now at least. I've wasted my whole day on a fruitless task. I should have known that word would have spread around the gentry. Their servants have all been warned off

101

having anything to do with me," James turned and raised his drink to the man who had offered him a place on his boat. "I'm much obliged to you, Thomas. I won't let you down."

"Give it time, son. Pat McGrother is well respected in our community and we all stand by him, isn't that so?" said one of the men, looking around the crowded room.

A chorus of cheers followed, as drinks were raised in a toast to James's uncle, but one voice was more subdued and one arm not lifted as high as the rest.

"I had best be getting home. I know it's early by my standards but if it means that Ma will leave me in peace it's worth it," John McDermott announced as he drained the last few drops of his porter.

"If you haven't learned to turn a deaf ear yet son, then you had better stay single. You'll be driven demented if you don't," said his father, smiling at the nods of agreement he received.

"Sure I owe you something for the drink tonight, don't I? She'll only be half as mad if one of us comes home sober," John said to his father, before heading towards the door.

On his way through the men, packed tightly into Paddy Mac's on account of a fundraising event held there earlier, John came face to face with James McGrother. There was an awkward silence as he stopped and stared at the latter, as if about to say something to him.

"If I was you, I would heed what your father said about the deaf ear, John. Are you still courting that young one from Ardee?" asked James. "I hear she has a tongue on her that could clip a hedge."

The young man smiled good naturedly at the joke being made at his expense and waved as he left the laughter behind him. The fresh air set his face tingling after the stuffy warmth of Paddy Mac's but instead of turning towards his own cottage, John headed in the opposite direction, a heavy weight bearing down on his conscience.

The house that loomed at the end of the road was in total darkness, not even the glow of a fire showing through the window. John was about to walk away, having lost his nerve, when the sound of coughing came from the trees at the side of the house.

"Is that you, Daniel?" the young man asked, peering into the shadows.

"No, it's not Daniel. That's the curse of getting old, son," a tall, slender middle-aged man walked towards him, "An interrupted night's sleep – and I daresay it won't be the last visit I make to the bushes before morning. I saw you with your father at the meeting tonight, does that mean you sympathize with the Brotherhood, or do you side with the Church against it?"

Matthew Clarke stood a good four inches taller than the young man in front of him. Finding himself facing his friend's father, John had the urge to turn on his heel and run but that would only arouse suspicion and cause more trouble in the long term.

"I was hoping to pay a visit with Daniel, is he ailing? It's not like him to leave so early when there's a good crowd in Paddy Mac's," John was thinking fast and avoided answering the question. "I take it he's asleep, if he's home at all. Your house is in darkness."

"Well now, I did wonder myself at why he accompanied me home. As you know, John, I haven't touched a drop in years and once the meeting was over there was no need for me to stay. I don't believe in tempting faith, son. Lizzie and the wee ones were asleep when we arrived so we went off to bed ourselves. Do you want me to wake up Daniel for you? Is it an urgent matter, or can it wait till morning?" asked Matthew.

John was tempted to have his friend woken up but realized that his own father would be home in an hour or so and would wonder what had become of him. He answered that it was not very important and could wait, then said goodnight.

As he watched the young man disappear into the dark night, Matthew Clarke couldn't help feeling that there was something very serious troubling John McDermott. Stepping into his cottage, he saw a shadow move away from the small window in the room and knew that his son had been watching. Whispering into the dark corner where Daniel lay on his bed, Matthew said he knew he was awake and he was to join him outside.

"That was your friend, John, looking to speak with you. What were you doing, hiding in the dark, instead of coming outside to join us?" asked Matthew.

"We had a difference of opinion earlier, that's why I left with you. I didn't want to have a row with him. It will have all blown over by the time the drink wears off."

"Was it over a woman, son? Do ye both have your eye on the same girl?"

Although his father teased him by asking such a question, Daniel felt relieved at what he saw as a good excuse for his behaviour.

"Now you have it. I didn't want to tell you for fear of the embarrassment it would cause me. I would rather you forgot about it and let us sort it out between ourselves," replied Daniel, letting out a long, slow breath.

"I would truly like to do that if I thought it was the reason for your trouble," his father replied, "But there is something more serious going on between you two that no girl could ever be the cause of. I'll not rest till you tell me what it is, son. You know what it means to keep a secret, as does every man at that meeting tonight. If this has anything to do with the Brotherhood you must tell me. If not, I'll leave you in peace."

Daniel could feel his resolve weakening and was beginning to regret not speaking with his friend while he had the chance. The strain on the face of James McGrother that evening had brought home to him how much the man was suffering at the incarceration of his uncle. John McDermott had been standing beside Daniel when James walked into Paddy Mac's and the two friends had exchanged concerned glances. There was no need to speak of what was on their minds, they knew what the other was thinking.

"It's only right that I should have a word with John first," said Daniel, "If he's in agreement, then we will confide in you, Da. Please don't ask me any more questions tonight. I'll wait until after Mass tomorrow to arrange a meeting for both of us with John. He might want his father to come, too."

"Don't involve his father just yet, son. That man's tongue is too easily loosened by drink and if this has anything to do with the Brotherhood, the less who know of it, the better," Matthew Clarke patted his son's back before turning to enter his cottage, "Well, I think we should get what little sleep is left to us before the rest of the house wakes up, don't you?"

Daniel nodded in agreement but knew there would be no sleep for him that night, after what had just passed between them.

CHAPTER EIGHTEEN

The failed uprising of the Young Irelanders in 1848 saw some of them going to America and others to France. James Stephens, John O'Mahoney and Michael Doheny, among them. Stephens came back to Ireland from Paris in 1858 and established the Irish Republican Brotherhood, a counterpart to the Fenian Brotherhood which had been formed in America by John O'Mahoney and Michael Doheny. They believed that armed insurrection was the only way to end British rule over Ireland and their members came to be known as Fenians.

It was to a secret meeting in a room at the back of Paddy Mac's that Matthew Clarke brought his son Daniel and his friend John McDermott. The young men had confided in him about certain activities that had been taking place in the locality – activities they were deeply involved in.

"Sit down, men," the voice of the man standing by the window was mellow but commanding.

Matthew had already explained to the young men that there would be no introductions as names were not important and better left unknown. As John and Daniel sat nervously waiting to be questioned, a dark figure outside moved across the window and seconds later a knock was heard on the door.

"All clear, sir. We're in our positions outside, ready for a signal," a boy who looked to be sixteen had entered the room.

"Good man, you can wait outside. This won't take long," said the mellow voice. "Your father tells me you have both been up to no good," this was said to John and Daniel as soon as the door closed.

"Well, to be fair to them, they were under the impression it was all in a good cause," said Matthew.

"Oh, the cause is indeed a very good one but their ignorance and naivety has created a big problem and led to a family's unnecessary suffering," the stranger with the mellow voice remained standing, his back to the window. "I know that both of you young men are aware of how the Brotherhood is organized and that names are not given outside of your own circle, and I am an outsider. However, I have been told about a local man who has been trying to gain a lot of favour and recognition in the Brotherhood because of the large amounts of money he has been contributing to the cause. This particular person is a man of little means, yet seems to have raised prolific funds from his trips to England, where he claims he receives money from supporters of the Brotherhood. He has the same name as the man you have been working for."

John and Daniel looked at each other, beads of sweat forming on their foreheads. A turf fire was burning but not so hot that it would cause them to overheat. Daniel looked anxiously at his father, who was standing to the right of the man speaking to them.

"Do you not realize that most of the money we raise comes from bonds sold to our supporters, and from donations generously made to the Brotherhood?" the voice was becoming less mellow. "Taking rifles and ammunition from soldiers and army barracks is acceptable. After all, they will be used upon our own people given half a chance. But robbing houses, no matter who the owner might be, is not something we encourage, especially when an innocent person is paying the price for it," the man's tone was much harsher as he finished his sentence.

"Sorry, sir. That was why we confided in my father," said Daniel. "Not because we thought what we had done was wrong, but because Pat McGrother is still being blamed for the theft."

The young men gave an account of how they had been instructed to retrieve stolen items, including Lord Devereux's missing silverware, from various hiding places around the county. They were told to bring them to the man they called Flannigan. They knew he travelled to England with the goods but after that they assumed the money went to into the Brotherhood's funds.

"When Pat McGrother was found with stolen goods on him, we were sure him and his nephew had been part of it," explained Daniel. "But Flannigan was the worse for drink the last time we met him and he laughed at his good fortune that Pat was in jail. When we asked what he meant by that, he said it was himself that had stolen the goods. He made a remark about the timing being perfect and said he would be calling a halt to the operation soon. We were warned not to breathe a word to anyone, as informers were everywhere and lives were dependant on our keeping quiet. I asked if my father knew about it and was told the only way to ensure a successful mission was if one hand didn't know what the other was doing. It seemed to make sense at the time, so we went along with it, thinking we were helping the fight for freedom. Isn't that so, John?"

"Daniel is telling the truth, sir. Flannigan brings trinkets over from England and sells them to the staff at the big houses. We think that's when he manages to steal whatever he finds lying around the kitchens. Now that he is suspected of lining his own pocket, we can see him for what he is, but at the time he seemed genuine. We only wanted to help the cause, sir, and Flanagan gave us an opportunity to do so – or so we thought," explained John. "If we had known what he was really up to we would never have gotten involved. You have to believe us, sir. Sure we never once took anything for ourselves. Did we, Daniel?" asked John.

Daniel shook his head and the sorry look on both their faces was enough to convince Matthew Clarke that his son and his friend were telling the truth about everything. Whether the man standing next to him was of the same mind was a different matter. Men had disappeared for a lot less, never to be heard of again and for the first time Matthew felt a stab of fear for his son's safety.

"As it turns out we have been watching Flannigan's movements in England. It appears that he is completely unaware of our suspicions, so the conversation we have had in this room must not reach anyone else's ears. Is that understood?" the question was directed at the two friends but Matthew Clarke joined with them in vigorously nodding his head.

"Good, good," the voice had returned to its mellow tone and the young men began to relax. "You two can go now, but I'd like you to stay behind, Clarke. I want to have a word with you in private."

When the older men were alone Matthew answered some questions about Flannigan. There was not a lot to tell as he had only arrived in the town a year before. His accent was more Monaghan than Louth and steps had been made to trace where he came from originally. In England he was known to visit the same house in Liverpool, every time he arrived there. It was believed that the woman and five children who lived in it were his family.

"What will happen to the boys? They meant no harm," asked Matthew.

"I think they have had enough of a scare but you must keep your eye on them, Clarke."

"I will to be sure and I won't give them a minute's peace. You have my word on that, sir. What about Flannigan?"

The man with the mellow voice smiled, "He thinks he's getting away with it but give him enough rope and he'll hang himself. When your son and his friend are no longer around, Flannigan will have to retrieve the bounty himself now, won't he?"

Matthew's heart skipped a beat at what was said, "What do you mean by 'no longer around,' sir? Surely you don't mean to harm them."

"Not at all, Clarke. Not at all. Here, have a seat," a chair was pulled out from a table in the centre of the room, "But for their own safety they must be sent away. You do see that, don't you?"

"How far? The west, or Cork maybe. Surely not to England, my wife won't be happy about that," said Matthew.

"I'm sorry, Clarke. Even further – to America."

Matthew jumped up from his seat, "You can't be serious. For how long?"

"Indefinitely, I'm afraid. There are a lot of men, and quite a few women, who have had to exile themselves because someone has been too careless or too foolhardy. The Brotherhood is in its infancy and will no doubt have many problems such as this one to deal with. We handle these situations as best we can, even when sacrifices must be made. Go home, man, and prepare your son and his friend for what lies ahead. As far as anyone else is concerned, and I include your good wife and your family in this, the boys have been offered work in America. They must be out of the country before Flannigan is dealt with. If they were to remain in Ireland or even England they will end up behind bars. Better that they live as free men in exile than prisoners of the Crown."

CHAPTER NINETEEN

The farewell party that John McDermott's parents had thrown in Paddy Mac's was a sad affair for Daniel Clarke. John had always dreamed of going to America and had been saving his money for such a day. Finding his fare had been paid and accommodation waiting for him, he gave his parents his savings to organize what was often called an *American Wake*.

Daniel, on the other hand, had never once thought of emigrating with his friend. His seasonal trips to England twice a year supplemented what he earned on his father's boat and that was how he had envisioned his future. In time he would have saved enough money to afford a wife and settled down to a life much like that of his parents.

"What are all the long faces for?" asked John as he approached the Clarke family, "Look, your two wee sisters are enjoying themselves, Daniel. Get out there and join the fun."

"If you will excuse us we'll be saying goodnight to you, John, I have a blinding headache and Matthew is going to walk me home," Lizzy Clarke embraced the young man, "Have a good life in America and watch out for each other – and don't forget to go to Mass of a Sunday. I'll see you in the morning, Daniel, I'm sure to be asleep by the time you get back to the house."

"Do you want me to fetch my parents, Mrs. Clarke? It's no trouble," asked John.

Matthew looked across the crowded floor, to where the McDermotts were dancing a set and said, "Leave them be, son. We will see them tomorrow at the quayside, when yourself and Daniel take your leave of us."

Daniel watched with a heavy heart as his parents walked away, his father's arm around his mother's waist. John stood beside him and elbowed his friend in the ribs. He couldn't understand why the Clarke's looked so downhearted.

"Aren't we the fortunate ones? Passage paid for and employment waiting for us. Sure what more could we ask for? Wait till you get there, Daniel, it won't take long for you to settle in and before you know it you will have saved up the fare for your Ma and Da to visit. They might like it so much, they will want to move over themselves. Come on and grab a partner before the night is over."

"You go on ahead, John. I'll be there in a minute, I just need some fresh air," said Daniel.

Outside, a group of men who had been talking quietly among themselves, stopped their conversation when Daniel sat nearby on the wall across from Paddy Mac's. After exchanging some pleasantries and wishing the young man well in America, the men went back to join the party. The air smelled of seaweed and as Daniel inhaled deeply, he tasted a trace of salt on his lips. The waves were lapping onto the sand behind him as he closed his eyes to savour all the smells and sounds of home.

"Do you mind if I join you Daniel?" James McGrother's quiet voice invaded the young man's thoughts.

"I was trying to set the sound of home firmly in my head, so when I'm away I can recall it whenever I feel the need to. Do you think I'm behaving like an old woman, James?" laughed Daniel.

"I do the same thing the night before I take the boat to England, every time I go. Some of us are not meant to leave, there's nothing wrong with that. Are you going because of your friendship with John McDermott?" asked James.

"That's as good a reason as any, isn't it?" replied Daniel. "Did you never think about going yourself, to America, I mean?"

"I had a friend once who begged me and Mary to go with him and his wife. He tried England for a while but America had a greater pull on him. We get a letter once or twice a year from him and in each one he still urges me to join him but I have never once been tempted – until now, that is."

"Do you mean because of your uncle? Is that why you would think of going?" asked Daniel.

"I can't bear to think of him trapped inside that place, away from his family. The children miss him sorely. No matter what he did, he's an old man who deserves to be shown some mercy. Would you not agree?"

"I would, James, I would. I'll pray for his release every night until I hear word that he's free. It won't be long until his case is heard. The magistrates are bound to go easy on him, on account of his age, I'm sure of it."

James stood and stretched his legs. The stamping of feet and clapping of hands in time to the music reminded him of the farewell parties his family held each time he left England to return home. He had brought Maggie and

Catherine to Paddy Mac's, as Mary had not been in the humour, electing to stay home with the younger children. James had spent most of the evening sitting on the wall looking out to sea, regretting the sale of his boat. He held out a hand to Daniel wishing him a safe voyage and a good life.

"I had best be getting my young one home but wild horses would not drag my sister away from that music," said James.

"I'll see that she gets home safe, no need to worry. I had better come in with you, John will be thinking I've left the country without him," laughed Daniel.

Matthew Clarke stood in the shadows watching his son return to the party with James McGrother. He had wanted to speak with Daniel in private and was making his way back, when he saw both men sitting together on the wall. Deciding it was better not to interrupt their conversation, Matthew waited until they had gone inside before entering himself and taking a seat at one of the tables.

He watched his son dancing a set and his heart ached at the false smile the young man was wearing. Matthew knew that it would be a very long time before they would see each other again, but that was easy enough to accept, he was a patient man and so was his son. It was the fact that Daniel did not want to go that made his parting hard to bear.

"Well Da, what are you thinking about? Are you wishing you were coming with me?"

Matthew looked up and realized his son was standing in front of him. The music had stopped and Daniel was holding out a jug.

"Go on, it's only lemonade. You have a thirsty look about you."

"Thank you, son. I came back to have a bit of time alone with you but you seem to be enjoying the company. I'll leave it till morning, before the rest of the family wake up. Your ma will be clinging to you like a barnacle until you step foot on the boat."

CHAPTER TWENTY

James followed the constable on duty to the cell that held his uncle. He had decided to lie to the old man by telling him that he had been able to get his boat back from the man he sold it to. Although he felt it was the right thing to do, James knew he would have to mention the lie when he next went to confession.

The young man's heart felt lighter at the prospect of giving his uncle the 'good news' about the boat and he called out to him as the door was unlocked. James was used to seeing the crumpled shape sitting in the corner of the cell every time he paid a visit. Pat McGrother always sat in the same place, he was there when his nephew arrived and he would return to it as he was leaving.

The constable told James that Pat had agreed to wash himself earlier that morning.

"I wonder what made him change his mind," said James.

"It's possible he could no longer bear his own stench," as this was not said in a sarcastic way, James smiled and agreed with the man.

"Or he might have imagined his wife rebuking him over it. He told me on my last visit that Aunt Annie was not too happy about the lodgings or the food," both men laughed at that and the constable locked the door, leaving them alone.

On this particular visit Pat seemed extra quiet, so James assumed he was asleep and sat down beside him on the edge of a straw-filled mattress, which his uncle had pulled into the corner to sit on.

"I bought the boat back from your man, Uncle Pat. What do you think about that then?"

There was no reply so James leaned in closer and repeated what he had just said. Pat remained perfectly still, as if in a deep sleep and James contemplated waking him up. If he didn't, then his uncle would think that no one had paid him a visit that day and that would be worse than disturbing his slumber.

"Uncle Pat, wake yourself up, our time is running out," James grabbed hold of the old man's jacket and shook him gently.

On feeling some movement, he let go of the fabric but was caught by surprise when Pat leaned away from him. James's hand shot out again and he just managed to halt his uncle's fall before his head connected with the floor. It was then that he realized something was very wrong. The coldness of the old man's hand when he grabbed hold of it sent a shiver down his spine and James shouted out to the constable to come and help him.

As soon as they lifted him up, both men knew that Pat was gone. The constable felt for a pulse but shook his head when none could be found. "I'm sorry," he said, then left to send for the prison doctor and a priest. James whispered a hurried prayer into his uncle's ear. The young man sat at the end of the wooden platform that Pat lay stretched out on and lifted the old fisherman's head onto his lap. Stroking the white beard and running his fingers through the equally white hair, James broke down and cried, begging for forgiveness. Try as he might, he could not control his grief, his heart was breaking. As James bowed his head, tears

119

landed on his uncle's glazed eyes and it looked
to him as if Pat was crying, too.

"Give my love to Aunt Annie," he whispered,
drawing his hand down the old man's face to
close his eyes. Something inside James changed
at that moment and it would be a long time
before he would recognize what it was.

CHAPTER TWENTY-ONE

William Harrington had managed to convince Lord Devereux of James McGrother's innocence in relation to the missing silverware. His uncle's confession of taking it in his confusion and not remembering what he had done with it appeared to satisfy the family of Freemont House. They had decided to offer a reward for information leading to its recovery. The solicitor was of the opinion that if it was hidden somewhere then it was only a matter of time before someone stumbled across it. As far as William Harrington was concerned the matter was closed.

However, the head constable had other ideas. He was convinced that the young fisherman, and possibly his wife and sister, had hidden the stolen goods and would eventually have to retrieve them. He was determined to keep a close eye on the family, ready to pounce at the first opportunity.

A pile of notes and coins lay in the centre of the desk between James and his solicitor. Both men had been staring silently at the money for a long time.

"I want you to be very sure about your decision, James. Think of how much rent that would cover,"

"I'll not change my mind, Mr. Harrington. I just need the amount that I have put into my pocket and the rest must go as payment towards the stolen silverware. Even if it should be found, I doubt that it would be handed over to its owner. I would rather be penniless than have the mention of my uncle's name cause a bitter taste in anyone's mouth," James said. "Will you not take some for yourself, after all the work you have done on our behalf?"

"I would if I had need of it but thank you for your offer, James. As far as your uncle's good name is concerned, I can tell you that whoever finds the hidden treasure will bless him for the rest of their lives. Although it will cover only a fraction of its value, this money will go a long way towards making amends to Lord Devereux and his family. I hope it will impress upon them the fact that you had nothing to do with the unfortunate actions of a confused old man. The receipt for your boat will prove to them the measures you have taken in order to raise this amount."

As they shook hands James asked William Harrington what made him take on cases that he knew he would never receive any payment for.

"I feel it's my Christian duty, and we have a common ground. It is as simple as that."

"But I'm a Catholic, Mr. Harrington, and a fisherman. What common ground do we share besides the fact that we are of a similar age?"

"More than you think. I'm Irish first and Protestant second. I have felt that way since childhood. Besides, we are both Christian are we not?"

James smiled and thanked the man once more for his kindness. The sun was struggling to get out from behind a cloud and the day looked promising. Heading towards the quays, he had one last stop to make before his return home.

When he eventually arrived at the door of his cottage, James was surprised to see his eldest child home from school. She was sitting beside one of the few rosebushes to survive the digging up of the garden by police, in their search for the missing silverware.

"Are you unwell, Catherine?" James lowered himself onto the grass beside her.

She shook her bowed head and when her father lifted her onto his lap he saw she had been crying.

"I miss him too, love, we all do. But he is in a better place now, sure you know that," said James.

"I was thinking of Mamó. She asked me to look after Dadó because she was too sick to do it herself and I promised her that I would. The next day she was dead," Catherine looked at her father through red-rimmed eyes. "I didn't mind him very well, did I?"

James wrapped his arms around his daughter, holding her close. He knew that no matter what he said, it would not change how she felt. He was carrying his own heavy weight of guilt, fearing that he had somehow brought on the death of his uncle by telling him that he had sold his boat. It was something he would regret for the rest of his life, and at that moment, James felt incapable of consoling his daughter.

"Well now, you are not the only one in this family that has failed in keeping their word. If the truth be known, it has been a year of broken promises. So dry up those tears, my love, and come into the house with me, I have some news for ye all," he stood Catherine up and held a hand out to her. "Here, give your poor father some help. My legs are stiff as boards."

The aroma of food cooking over the fire made James aware of his hunger and he lifted the lid of a large, black pot to peer inside.

"I killed one of the hens. She was getting old and only good for the pot. Besides, the children could do with a bit of meat, James, and you haven't taken up any offers of a place on a boat lately, have you?"

Mary had a hard edge to her voice that made James think twice about telling them his news. An old chipped plate full of bread sat in the centre of the table surrounded by bowls waiting to be filled with the stew. James felt there was something wrong with the scene before his eyes. He knew that, apart from the baby, only four members of the family were home, with two of the children still at school, and yet there were six of Annie's wooden bowls on the table.

"Why have you got extra bowls set out, Mary, are you expecting visitors?" no sooner were the words out of his mouth than James gasped in shock.

"Bless us and save us," he said, "What are you doing with those two bowls, Mary? Have we not had enough trouble as it is over them?"

"I thought that would be your reaction. I said as much myself," Mary shot a scathing look at her sister-in-law, "Is that not so, Maggie?"

The older woman had been playing with baby Brigid and continued to bounce the laughing child on her knee as she spoke, "They belong together and don't either of you dare bring them back. I paid for them with my own money and her ladyship up at the big house knows where they are this time, so we will have no trouble from her. Now, this poor wee child is about to perish with the hunger. Are we going to eat that unfortunate hen or not?"

The uneasy silence throughout the meal was killing James but he wanted everyone to finish eating before informing them of a decision he had made that could very well tear them apart. He watched as Catherine slowly drained her bowl of every last drop and no sooner had it landed back on the table, than he blurted out his news.

"We are moving to Sunderland in a fortnight's time. When Owen came over for Pat's funeral he told me there was work to be had in one of the foundries, if I went over within the month. Once I step foot on that boat, I'm gone for good, I'm not coming back. We can stay at Maggie's for a while, until we find a place of our own. The tickets are paid for and that's final so ye had better prepare for a new life. I won't be persuaded to change my mind about this," James hardly took a breath as he spoke and heaved a sigh of relief once the words were out.

"Well now, ye can stay at my house for as long as ye like. I won't be coming with ye and if I have to move in with one of the neighbours here, so be it," Maggie bounced the baby onto Mary's lap and stormed out of the house.

"Me too," cried Catherine, running after her aunt.

Mary calmly wiped Brigid's face with the end of her apron, without saying a word. James was unable to look at his wife. He waited for her to berate him and try to change his mind but instead, all he could hear was the soft humming of a tune she always sang to the children.

"You're very quiet, Mary. What have you got to say about my decision?"

"I only have one problem with it, James. It galls me that you made *your* decision without first confiding in your *wife* and then you had the bad manners to surprise her with it, in front of your sister *and* your daughter," Mary placed Brigid on her father's lap. "Apart from that, I will be only too happy to put this place and its painful memories behind me. As far as I am concerned, the sooner I step foot off this sorry island, the better. That's what I have to say about *your* decision, James McGrother."

CHAPTER TWENTY-TWO

James had taken to walking with his children, Catherine, Thomas and Mary-Ann, along the roads in the surrounding countryside. They crossed fields and streams, while he told them stories relating to the different landmarks they encountered along the way. Although he could no longer live in his homeland, James did not want his children to forget where they came from. He hoped that in their lifetime Ireland would be a much better place for them to return to. A country with something to offer, instead of always taking until there was nothing left except the grave or a boat. These were the thoughts the young father mulled over while he waited to follow in the footsteps of his brothers and sisters, a decade after their own departure.

"Here's as good a place as any to eat our meal. Sit down there and rest for a while, Mary-Ann is struggling to keep up on those poor wee legs of hers," said James.

The children sat and ate potatoes that their father had carried in a cloth bag, tied to the end of a stick and placed across his shoulder.

"Am I like The Blind McCourt, Daddy, you know, the poet?" asked Thomas.

"Why do you ask that, have you taken to writing verse?"

"I wrote a poem about us leaving our house and the Master read it out to the class. He said I might even be as good as An Dall MacCuarta."

"When was this, Thomas? Does your mammy know about it? She would be very proud of that, son?"

"Mammy told us not to tell you and said that Thomas was to stop writing such nonsense. She said the Master was filling our heads with things that would have us wanting to be above our station – whatever that means," Catherine mumbled through a mouthful of potato.

Although James understood why Mary had said such a thing, he was annoyed that she had made little of the boy's effort. The girls had wandered off chasing each other through the long grass but Thomas was still sitting beside his father, enjoying the male company.

"Ah, your mammy is too busy with the trials and tribulations of life to pay heed to the visions of a poet, Thomas."

"What does that mean, Daddy?"

"You'll understand when you find yourself with a family to feed and a roof to keep over your heads. The Blind McCourt often stayed at the house of Aunt Annie's grandfather, or so the story goes."

"I know, Daddy. Mamó used to tell us that story, too. She said he was put out of his home with his family when he was only a young boy and went from village to village for the rest of his life, with his songs and poems. If I don't become a doctor, I think I might do that instead."

"Well, if you don't get work I suppose you can always try it. People used to give McCourt food and lodgings in exchange for entertaining them with his words," James was not one to trample on a young boy's dreams. "We had better be getting back, son, our walk took us a lot further than I intended today."

Once the children had gone to bed that evening, Mary sat by the fire in what the family referred to as 'Pat's chair' and began to mend some clothes, in preparation for their trip to England.

"I'll not have us looking like a bunch of ragamuffins when we land across the water," she said stabbing James's good shirt with a needle.

"I hope you're not getting above your station, love," said James, smiling to himself.

"Why would you say such a thing? I just want us to look decent and not like the bedraggled, uncivilized Irish beggars that people over there expect to see coming off the boat.

James's smile left his face as his stomach turned, "Do not belittle your own kind like that, woman. A person is not uncivilized just because they lack decent clothing and a livelihood. We are all at the mercy of circumstance and misfortune, as you well know," James leaned forward and deliberately spat into the fire. "Sorry, Mary, am I being uncivilized? Have I offended your genteel nature?"

As he stood up, he pushed his chair back with such force, it toppled over. Leaving it where it lay, James put on his cap and jacket and left his wife sitting open mouthed by the fire. She had never heard such venom in his voice in all the years they had known each other. That it should be directed towards herself, his own wife, was even worse. Mary sat for a long time after the door had been slammed shut, staring into the flames, her sewing abandoned.

By the time Maggie got back from Kitty Carroll's the fire had died down and Mary was sitting in the dark, not even a candle lit.

"I'm happy that I can do my own mending, if you've been sewing in the dark. What ails you?"

Mary told her sister-in-law what James had said and how it had affected her.

"Ah, he was only taking out his frustrations on you. Sure isn't that why we get married in the first place?" Maggie said as she set right the upturned chair.

"It wasn't what he said but the way he said it. I've never heard such coldness in his voice before, it froze me to the spot," Mary shivered. "Who says we get married out of frustration? That's not the reason I wed James."

Maggie laughed, "No, nor I. Us women marry out of love. As for the men – do you not remember your courting days, Mary? Him wanting a wee bit more and you fending him off, fighting against your own temptation at the same time."

"Hush woman, that's your brother you're speaking of. You should be ashamed of yourself," Mary admonished, slightly embarrassed at the forwardness of Maggie's words.

Both women stared at the glowing turf in silence, until Mary burst out laughing.

"Oh Maggie, I have to admit, what you say is true about his frustration. I don't know how many times James told me he was driven demented, and that our wedding day could not come soon enough for him."

"Wedding *night* you mean, Mary. Sure it was the same for me. I've been widowed so long now that I have forgotten what it's like to have to answer to a man, and I fully intend on keeping things that way."

"So you'll not change your mind about coming with us then?" asked Mary.

"If I move back there I will wither away and die. Kitty Carroll and her daughter told me they will be glad of the company and that I can stay with them for as long as I like. James won't be too happy about that, will he?" said Maggie.

Mary remarked that nothing seemed to make her husband happy any more. It was why she had agreed with his decision about moving to England. The death of his uncle, alone and confused, separated from his family, had changed James from a warm-hearted man to one with a cold and bitter nature. Mary feared he would get worse if they stayed and had thought about moving back to Monaghan, but the only family either of them had was the one across the water. What was left of her own kin had settled in America and apart from a handful of letters received over the years, Mary knew nothing about them.

"A fresh start is what we need, Maggie. My only fear is that it will not suit the children over there. The air is heavy and stale and there are too many people crowded into every street. I worry how Mary-Ann will fare with her delicate nature."

"Rose will take care of her if she's ailing, like she did with my youngest. That woman could have been a doctor if she were born a man and to a wealthy family," said Maggie.

"You are quite the healer yourself," Mary patted her sister-in-law's hand. "I have a lot to thank you for, Maggie, and I will miss you sorely. I intend to keep begging you to come with us, right up until we board that boat. James still has your ticket," she stood up, placing her sewing on the table. "I'm going to sleep upstairs with you and the children tonight. It would be better for James if I don't see him when he gets home and I will feel less bitterness towards him after a night's sleep."

"I will be up shortly, Mary. Leave Brigid here with me for now, the wee mite is fast asleep. I'll bring her to you if she wakes up looking to be nursed."

******

Paddy Mac knew better than to put a drink up in front of Matthew Clarke. The last time he had done that, every stick of furniture in the place had been reduced to firewood. Some men should never touch alcohol and he was one of them. Paddy watched as Matthew sat down on a bench beside James McGrother, who had been in a sour mood since storming through the door earlier that evening.

"I called in to tell some of the men about a bit of labouring work, James, are you interested?"

The young man looked at Matthew with glazed eyes and shook his head slowly.

"Much obliged for the offer but the next time I break sweat earning a wage, it will be on foreign soil," James slurred, raising his drink in salute.

"Can I give you a word of advice?" Matthew waited until James nodded his head. "Don't be so quick to look for comfort in the bottom of a tankard. All you will find there is grief and you know very well how that feels."

"Well now, Mr. Clarke, I'm grateful for your concern about my grief, and yes, I do know what that feels like – as does every man here this evening, including your good self. But I am not looking to ease that particular pain, I have had plenty of practice with that already," James took a long drink. "No, Matthew, what I cannot stand is the guilt and remorse that I am unable to shake off. Those feelings are there every cursed minute of my day. They even invade my dreams by night."

Knowing how difficult it would be to reason with a man who had been drinking for the evening, Matthew placed a hand on his young friend's shoulder.

"Time heals all things eventually, James, if you allow it to. When you are settled with your family across the water things will get better for you, mark my words."

"I will be too busy labouring over there to spend much time dwelling on the past. I know you are concerned to see how often I come in here, but it is the only way I can get a night's sleep."

"I know, James, I know. Well, if you change your mind about the labouring, we will be meeting up at Father Marmion's, it was him that put the work my way. Sure we can get a blessing on our day while we are at it. It would do you good to be there but I won't press you about it," Matthew held out his hand.

"You're a fine man, Matthew Clarke, and a good neighbour," James grasped a hand that was as calloused as his own from years of fishing, labouring and working the bog.

"Goodnight James."

As Matthew walked out of Paddy Mac's he felt as if a mountain of guilt had been heaped upon his shoulders. It was unnerving how close he had come to telling the young fisherman the truth about his uncle. Giving out information like that, no matter how good the intention was, could get a man killed. Matthew had been assured that Flannigan would get what he deserved and Pat McGrother's name would finally be cleared. The fact that justice would be served too late for the old man's family, left a bitter taste in Matthew's mouth. Add to that the forced exile of his own son, and it took all of his will power not to hunt down Flannigan and throttle him until he had squeezed every last breath from the wretched man's body.

CHAPTER TWENTY-THREE

Rose looked across the Sunday dinner table at her husband and nodded. They had agreed that James needed a fatherly talking to and it had been difficult to find the time to do it with both men working six long days a week.

"James, I fancy a walk in the evening air. We can't hear ourselves think in this noise," Owen said over the chatter of their families.

"Maybe we should bring the children with us, give the women a bit of peace for a while," James knew his brother was worried about him but was not in the mood to share his troubles.

"You have been here more than a month now, and we have hardly said two words to each other. I want to spend some time alone with my youngest brother, is that too much to ask?"

Mary moved the children away from the table and sat them on a bench to hand out some biscuits she had made that day. There was a thin layer of sugar icing on the top, a rare treat, and whoops of joy filled the parlour.

"We can go for a walk and leave you two here to enjoy each other's company. It would be good to tire out these rascals and get them to bed early for a change," suggested Rose, "Come on, Mary, take hold of some of these sticky hands."

Once they were alone in the quiet house together, Owen was at a loss for words. The two brothers made small talk about their work, the weather and local news, avoiding anything personal. Eventually, with nothing left to discuss they fell silent. The ticking of the clock on the mantelpiece seemed to get louder, reminding Owen that their time alone was running out.

"Are you missing Uncle Pat? You never talk about him and if anyone brings his name up, you change the conversation or make an excuse to leave," said Owen.

"Of course I miss him, and Aunt Annie too. Just because I don't want to dwell on the past doesn't mean I've forgotten about them. Has Mary been complaining about me again? It's all that woman is capable of these days, you should get Rose to have a word with *her*. It's not *me* who needs the advice."

"Mary has never spoken against you, at least not to me, James. She may have confided in Rose, but that's what women do. I'm not blind I can see things for myself, and I don't need someone else to point out to me there is something very wrong with my brother. Even Peter has remarked on it."

"Is this about me refusing to go out with ye to the Peacock? Did I not tell you that I have been overly fond of the drink lately and of my need to avoid such places? Sure ye both know I was never much of a drinker," snapped James.

The irritation in his brother's voice told Owen that James was once again shutting him out. He glanced at the clock and knew that their wives and children would be home shortly.

"I'm not talking about drink, James. Can you not see the change in yourself? Where has my good natured brother gone? The one who was always even tempered, slow to anger and quick to smile," asked Owen.

"If you see Uncle Pat in the next life, ask him his opinion of me and my *'good nature'* and see what *he* has to say about it."

"He knew it was not your fault that he drew his last breath in jail. Why do you think he would blame you, James?"

"That is not what he held against me, he knew I was doing my best to have him released. It was the boat. You should have seen his face when I told him I had sold the boat. It was as if I had punched him in the gut. I cannot get that image out of my head, it will stay with me for the rest of my days."

"You have always looked up to Uncle Pat, haven't you James?" said Owen.

The young man nodded his head, "That's what makes it so hard, knowing how much I disappointed him."

"He wasn't perfect. Pat had his own regrets about mistakes he made when he was a young man. Big mistakes, much more serious than anything you think you may have done to him."

"Like what? Tell me then, what did he do that was so bad?" asked James.

Owen struggled with how much he should reveal to his brother about a secret he had kept from the rest of the family for many years.

"It's the reason why he left the county to go live in Blackrock. Why do you think he never came to visit us?" asked Owen.

"What are you trying to say? Does Peter know? Am I the only one unaware of this terrible thing Uncle Pat is supposed to have done?" asked James.

"I'm the only one besides Da and Uncle Pat who knows what happened. I remember waking

137

up one night and seeing the door open, so I crept over and peeked outside. Pat was crying and telling Da that it was his fault Annie had lost her baby."

"Annie had a baby, why did she never say? When was this?" James was shocked.

"It was a long time before you were born. I would have been about the age of ten, old enough to know what they were talking about. None of us children knew Annie was with child but maybe our parents did. I don't think that any of the neighbours were aware of it either, I don't remember it ever being mentioned outside of that night," Owen went quiet as Rose and the children burst through the door.

"Mary brought your wee ones home, James. Mary-Ann was getting tired," said Rose.

"Well then, Owen, let's be having that walk," James grabbed his cap and jacket.

The men said goodnight to the children and Owen warned them to be asleep by the time he returned. As they fell into step, he told James about a dispute over a field that Pat had been involved in with a neighbour. The man was later found dead at the bottom of a rocky hill.

"It happened the same night that Annie lost her baby," said Owen. "Everyone thought the poor man must have tripped and banged his head on the rocks. He had been drinking earlier that evening."

"Are you speaking of Thomas Gartlan's father? What makes you think Pat had anything to do with that?" asked James.

"Because that's what I heard him tell Da. He said he couldn't keep it to himself any longer. Pat had gone looking for Gartlan and when he found him they got into a fierce row. Unbeknownst to Pat, Annie had followed him when he left the house, on account of the temper he was in. She rushed in between them when they came to blows. Pat said she took them both by surprise and got knocked off her feet. She rolled down the hill and landed hard against a rock, full on her belly, James."

"And lost the baby."

"Aye. When Pat helped her up they both noticed Gartlan lying at the foot of the hill, his head in a pool of blood. He died of a cracked skull and there was nothing they could do for him. Annie was having pains and Pat carried her home. They told no one about the fight and next morning the body was discovered."

"So why did Uncle Pat have to leave? Surely nobody suspected him, or was he seen by someone? Anyway, it was an accident," said James.

"To my knowledge, there was never a finger pointed at Pat, otherwise people would still be talking about it today. The night he told Da about the accident, he said he'd be leaving with Annie by the end of the week. He knew if he stayed he would never be able to keep it secret from the man's family. Pat told Da that he would not hold it against him if he decided to turn him in."

"A man would never do such a thing to his own brother, even if it was to ease his conscience," said James.

"Pat would have ended up in Van Diemen's Land for sure. People were already beginning to say how fortunate it was for him that Gartlan had taken a tumble and settled the dispute over the field by doing so. I'm sure it was said in jest but it made it harder for Pat to bear, so the only thing for him to do was leave."

"Knowing how soft Pat was, I can imagine the guilt he must have carried all those years – and yourself, Owen, sure you were only a child. Did you not think to tell Da you knew of their secret?"

"What? And get the living daylights beaten out of me for spying on them? No, James, it was something I should never have overheard and I was prepared to keep it to myself until my last breath."

James was deep in thought as he walked in silence alongside his older brother. Owen gave him sideward glances, trying to read his face in the dim light. When they reached Bridge Street, Saint Mary's church loomed ahead, light spilling out through its open doors.

"Will we go in and say a wee prayer for Pat?" suggested Owen.

When James followed him inside, he saw rows of people kneeling in the pews beside the confession box. It crossed his mind that he should tell the priest about the great guilt he carried around with him, but the thought was quickly dismissed. James lit a candle and knelt in front of it, intending to say a decade of the rosary. Instead of chanting the familiar prayers he had grown up with, he found himself talking quietly to his uncle. James asked if he could be forgiven for selling the boat that had meant so much to both of them.

Watching his brother kneeling in front of the rows of burning candles, Owen reflected on the secret he had just shared. He had said his own quick prayer that James would not hold it against him, either for passing on such a burden, or for the years he kept it to himself.

James finally lifted his head and nodded at his brother, before walking out of the church. As he caught up, Owen saw him wipe a sleeve across his face and remained a few steps behind, until he was sure the young man had regained his composure.

"I was thinking back there about Uncle Pat's last days in jail," said James. "I was so incensed with him at how easily he accepted his fate. Now that you have told me his secret, I think I understand why he felt that way. In his mind it must have seemed like he was doing penance for a sin he committed a long time ago."

"Then you won't hold it against me for telling you, or for keeping it from the rest of the family till now?" asked Owen.

"Of course not, but I think it's something that should remain just between the two of us. What good would come of sharing it now? We don't want anyone thinking badly of Uncle Pat, do we?" James held out a hand to his brother. "Our secret, agreed?"

Owen was more than happy to shake on it.

CHAPTER TWENTY-FOUR

Three sharp knocks on the door had Thomas running to open it while his mother dished up breakfast for his younger sisters. Catherine had left the house with her father two hours earlier, as James insisted on escorting his daughter to work before he began his own day's labouring. Rose had found employment for her niece as a scullery maid, in the home of one of the doctors at the hospital. Although she worked Monday to Saturday and a half day Sunday, the doctor and his wife did not insist on Catherine being a live-in domestic.

Rose had promised to see to it that Catherine arrived every morning at five o'clock to do her chores, the first one of the day being to light the stove before the cook woke up. By five o'clock in the evening, Catherine was finished for the day and on Sundays worked until ten o'clock in the morning, allowing her to go to Mass with her family. For the first few weeks, the poor girl spent most of her Sunday afternoons in an exhausted sleep.

"Who was that at the door, son?" asked Mary.

Thomas was walking across the parlour, reading the front page of a paper.

"It's the Dundalk Democrat, Ma. There was nobody at the door when I opened it but the paper was lying on the step."

"Let me see," said Mary, holding out her hands.

She opened the pages wide to scrutinize each image displayed but nothing stood out as unusual to her.

"Maybe someone from the street was given it and left it for your Da. I'll put it up here on the mantelpiece for when he gets home from work. If you don't get a move on soon, you'll be in trouble with Mr. Feeney for being late. There's many a boy waiting to take your place in his workshop."

"I know, Ma, I know. You don't have to keep reminding me, but Mr. Feeney says he would find it hard to find a boy my age who reads as well as I do. He says it was my literary skills that secured my position."

"Hark at you and your fancy words, mind you don't get too big for your boots, son. Here, take your food and be off with you," Mary ruffled Thomas's dark brown hair and watched from the doorway as he bolted up the street.

"Morning Mary, your young lad off to work then? He'll go far, that one, mark my words," one of the neighbours called out as she passed by.

"I was just telling him he's getting too big for his boots, so don't you go praising him to his face too often," Mary laughed, "But I'm much obliged for your kind words."

As the day wore on, the routine of the small courtyard that was home to the McGrother families helped Mary to cope with her homesickness. She had not expected to feel such a strong pull for Ireland, especially six months later. It was her husband that should have been longing to return. James could hardly bare to visit a town, never mind live in one and yet he seemed to have settled in without a word of complaint. Mary, on the other hand, always found something negative to say about their new life. That evening's annoyance was the smog hanging over the houses, the smoke from the fires trapped by the cold, damp winter air.

A rasping cough came from one of the children upstairs and Mary looked up from her sewing to glance at the ceiling.

"Mary-Ann's health is getting worse, I think I'll ask Rose to give her something for that cough. The air in this place is poisoning the poor wee thing," Mary looked across at James.

"Aye, she sounds bad, right enough. We should have a good breeze overnight to help freshen the air. If not, keep her indoors tomorrow," replied James as he carried on reading. "You say Thomas didn't see who left this paper."

Mary shook her head and listened as the news from home was read out to her. It was comforting to know that life was going on just as it always had and no big changes seemed to have taken place in the parish. James went very quiet and when Mary asked him what was wrong, he ignored her by carrying on reading to himself.

"James, what is it. Did somebody die? Tell me."

The young man looked up from the page he was reading and his face was so pale it caused Mary to reach out and check his forehead.

"Merciful heavens, are you ill? You're as white as a sheet," she got no answer. "James, tell me what you've read. What is it?"

Mary snatched the paper from her husband and her eyes scanned every inch of the page until she saw a circle drawn around one of the paragraphs.

"Is this what has you in such a state," she held out the paper. "Tell me what is says, James. You're frightening me. Has somebody died? Who is it?"

James took the newspaper from Mary's hands and looked once more at the words that had made his heart race.

"A body was discovered in the back yard of a house in Linen Hall Street on Thursday last. Neighbours identified the remains as that of a man called Flannigan. In his pocket was found two silver teaspoons. They have been identified by Lord Devereux as part of the collection of silverware reported missing from Freemont House." James paused to glance at Mary. *"It appears that Flannigan, who was reeking of alcohol, must have broken his neck in a fall while climbing over a six foot high wall – the gate being bolted at the time. A search of the house proved fruitless, until a slab of concrete was lifted in the back yard and a crate containing stolen goods was discovered."*

"So Pat's name can be cleared at last. Oh, James, that's good news, surely. Don't you think?"

"Too late for Uncle Pat, though, isn't it? I had better tell the rest of the family about this," James put on his jacket. "Maybe Owen or Peter will know how this paper found its way onto my doorstep."

Rose poured tea into Owen's cup as they waited for James to return to their house with Peter. They were puzzled as to what kind of news could have him so agitated. As soon as the

145

two men walked through the door Owen began to question his younger brother about the fuss he was making.

"Look at this," James spread the paper across the table and stabbed at it with his finger.

None of them were able to read but looked at the words anyway.

"Here, see this?" James was pointing to the circled paragraph. "I didn't put this mark here, it was there when I opened the page. Someone left this paper on my doorstep this morning. Do any of you know how it got there?"

They shook their heads and Owen again asked what all the fuss was about.

"I think ye need to sit down before I read out what it says," James responded.

When he had finished, there was a moment's silence, until Peter brought up the subject of the money from his boat that James had left with his solicitor, "Maybe you can get your money back now, James."

"This doesn't prove that Uncle Pat was innocent. Think about it, they will say that he supplied this man Flannigan with the stolen goods in exchange for money. What I am more concerned about, is finding out who sent me this paper. Rose, take this money," James placed some coins on the table. "Will you send a telegram to Maggie tomorrow, before you go to work?"

When his sister-in-law assured him she would, James continued. "I will write out exactly how it should be worded. I need Maggie to find out if Mr. Harrington still has the money in his safe, although I doubt it. When I last spoke with him, I made it clear that he was to hand it over to Lord Devereux."

"Are you regretting your decision now, James?" asked Owen.

"If this man Flannigan had the Devereux silverware, then yes, I do regret it, because I know for a certainty that Pat would have had nothing to do with such an unsavoury character. I think we might have done our poor old uncle a great injustice, in being too quick to believe that he had been stealing in his state of confusion."

"Do you think one of the neighbours left this paper on your doorstep?" asked Rose.

"They would have sent one of their young ones with it or at least stopped to say 'good morning' and not run off like that. No, whoever left it didn't want to be seen. That's the worry of it," said James.

"You don't suppose it was that constable with the grudge against you? He could have arranged to have it delivered," Peter suggested.

James agreed with his brother, saying that it was the first thing that came to mind when he read the news. "That's why we need to get Maggie to find out what the story behind this is. Flannigan's death is very convenient for me now, isn't it? And that's how the police will view it. But seeing as I had nothing to do with it, who else is it convenient for?"

"It could be that it was purely an accident, like the paper says, James. Let's not worry too much about this yet until we've asked the neighbours if it was left by any of them. We should know by this time tomorrow and Rose will have sent the telegram off to Maggie," said Owen.

"Bless her heart, the poor woman will think one of us has died when she gets it. Telegrams seldom carry good news," said Rose.

CHAPTER TWENTY-FIVE

It was the first time Maggie had been in William Harrington's office. Every time she looked at the telegram her hands shook and the young clerk noted her nervousness. He asked if she would like some tea but Maggie declined the offer. She was afraid it would spill over if she tried to steady a cup in the state she was in.

"Not bad news, I hope," the young man said, referring to the telegram.

"I thought somebody had died when I got it," laughed Maggie, "I'm still not over the shock. But it's not bad news, just worrying. I'm sure Mr. Harrington will know what to do."

No sooner had she said his name than the door to his office opened and he escorted an elderly, well dressed lady through the waiting area and into the hallway. A few minutes later the solicitor was back, instructing his clerk to organize some paperwork for him to sign later.

"Well, Margaret McGrother isn't it? Come inside and tell me what this is all about," he said.

Maggie quickly stood and followed Mr. Harrington into his office.

"Did my clerk offer you some tea?" he asked, holding out a chair for her.

"He did indeed, but it's a wee bit early for tea, if you don't mind, sir," Maggie still didn't trust herself not to spill it, "And it's O'Neill, sir. I was McGrother before I got married, but please call me Maggie."

"Yes, of course. How may I be of service?" Mr. Harrington asked.

Placing the telegram on the desk in front of her, Maggie explained what it was about as the solicitor read it for himself. The reference to the Dundalk Democrat and a page number had him confused.

"I went to Paddy Mac's and asked him to have a look through the paper in question. He can read himself and keeps a pile of newspapers on hand for his customers," Maggie took something from her pocket. "Paddy tore this out of Saturday's Democrat, so I could show it to you."

The solicitor took the piece of newspaper being held out to him by a shaking hand and read it.

"I know there's something very wrong with this, I can feel it in my bones, Mr. Harrington. I'm sure James does, too."

"I have not been made aware of this by the head constable. He should have informed me by now, as it involves one of my cases. Do you have an address for James so that I may contact him?"

"Thank you, Mr. Harrington. I knew you would know what to do. James is living in my house over in England, there's only my eldest boy left in it."

"Good, good," the solicitor stood and gestured for Maggie to follow him to the door. "My clerk will write down the details. Leave this with me, Maggie. I will be in touch as soon as I have news for you and if you, yourself, should hear of anything, please do not hesitate to inform me. I shall bid you good day for now, Mrs. O'Neill."

Maggie thanked Harrington again as she left his office to give his clerk the contact details for her brother. Stepping back into the busy street, she caught sight of Matthew Clarke standing by an ass and cart, and crossed over to speak with him.

"Are you minding it for someone, Matthew?" Maggie said, stroking the animal's head.

"She's mine. I just bought her and the cart this morning," said Matthew. "Lizzie is to meet me here before we head home. Do you want to come back with us, Maggie? Or do you have to stay in town?"

"I would be much obliged for the ride home, thank you. I suppose Lizzie and your girls will no longer have to carry heavy creels of fish to market, now that ye have some transport, will they?"

Matthew Clarke smiled and said it was as much his wife's idea to get the ass and cart as it was his.

"I can get more work, too, by having a cart. I've been saving for a long time to get this and it might never have happened only for the money our Daniel sends home."

"How is Daniel? I trust he's settled in well by now," asked Maggie as Matthew helped her up onto the cart.

"He's happy enough for someone who was so attached to home. Sure he isn't the first to leave and he won't be the last, Maggie. He's in good company over there anyway, and from what I can tell, he's behaving himself. A man can't ask more than that from a son, can he?"

A thought struck Maggie as Matthew was speaking of emigration, "You can read, can't you? Did you see that bit of news in the

Democrat about the man in Liverpool who was found dead with the Devereux silver on him?"

"No, I didn't. When did that happen?" Matthew had already heard the news, but didn't let on.

"It was in Saturday's Democrat. Someone showed it to James and he sent me a telegram letting me know. I've just been to Mr. Harrington, his solicitor, about it."

"Maggie, how are you?" Lizzie Clarke had arrived and climbed up beside her husband.

While the women chatted, Matthew was deep in thought. Every so often, at the mention of his name, he would nod his head then get back to what was bothering him. He felt sure it was not by accident that Flannigan had come to a sorry end, it had been on the cards for a long time. It was common knowledge among the neighbours that the head constable had a grudge against the McGrothers. Matthew feared that the incident in Dundalk might just add more fuel to the fire and make things even worse.

"The longer they are over there the less chance there'll be of them coming back. Isn't that so, Matthew?" said Lizzie.

"Who? The boys?" asked Matthew, his train of thought interrupted once more.

"No, we were speaking of James and Mary and their wee ones. Maggie was saying she lives in hope of them coming back to us. What do you think?"

"If there's regular work to be had over there, it could be a big mistake on James's part, bringing his family back here. He doesn't strike me as being a foolish man," Matthew noticed how silent both women had become at his words. "But he's your brother, Maggie, you know him better than I do. I was speaking on how I would feel about it, for myself and my own family."

Lizzie was surprised at what she heard, she knew that her husband would never leave for good. Every time he went to England for seasonal work he counted the days until his return home.

"Why Matthew Clarke, you're the one always saying 'I would rather be poor here than rich over there.' I don't believe for one minute that you would trade places with James McGrother, even if we lost the roof over our heads," Lizzie turned to look at their passenger. "We could be evicted and sleeping in the ditch and this man here would be telling me and the wee ones how fortunate we were to have fresh air to breathe," she laughed.

"Begging your pardon, Lizzie, but I would have to agree with your husband about that. Until you have lived over there in those crowded streets and tasted the thick vile air on a foggy day, you will never truly be thankful for what you have here," said Maggie.

"Sure don't they have countryside over there, too? With clean air, just like here? Take a trip up to Dublin, the pair of ye, and see how fresh the air is. Or Belfast, even worse, with all those factories. The way I see it, if you want a regular wage you must be prepared to put up with things that may not be to your liking – or taste."

Matthew laughed at his wife's tirade, "Now we've started her off on one of her speeches, Maggie. We'll have sore heads by the time we get home. Look, even the ass's ears are twitching."

Lizzie gave her husband a good-natured slap on the back of his head, knocking his cap off. The three of them laughed and their conversation took on a much lighter tone for the rest of the journey, until they reached Kitty Carroll's cottage. Outside the house stood a jaunting car, its driver adjusting the horse's bridle. As they came to a halt, the Clarkes and Maggie were surprised to see the head constable step out from behind the animal.

"Constable Armstrong I hope it's not bad news that has you on Mrs. Carroll's doorstep," Matthew said as he helped the women down from the cart.

"It's not Mrs. Carroll I'm here to see."

"It must be me so. To what do I owe the honour?" asked Maggie.

"Have you heard from your brother lately?" asked Armstrong.

"As a matter of . . ." Maggie began her answer.

"And what does that have to do with you?" Matthew interrupted.

"Were any of you acquainted with the man who was found dead in Linen Hall Street, who happened to have some items of stolen silverware on him at the time?"

Everyone shook their heads and Matthew looked directly into the policeman's eyes, "Drinking and climbing are best kept separate, would you not agree, Constable Armstrong?"

"News travels fast, doesn't it? His body was only discovered a few days ago," was the sarcastic reply.

"Some of us are well able to read a newspaper," said Maggie.

"Of course you are, your brother included. I'm sure he's heard the news himself by now. So, to get back to my question, was this Flannigan fellow a friend of your brother's, by any chance?" asked the constable.

"I never heard of the man before now, nor has James, I can assure you," Maggie was getting annoyed. "He was not the sort of person any of my family would be acquainted with."

"I believe you received a telegram this morning, I trust the news was not bad. How are all the McGrothers faring across the water?"

"Would you care for a cup of tea, Constable Armstrong? We are all gasping with the thirst," said Matthew, quickly changing the subject.

"Indeed we are," Lizzie agreed. "Come woman, show a bit of hospitality to your visitors," and she dragged Maggie into the house before she had a chance to say another word.

The two men stood outside the door, eyes locked on each other. Matthew kept a blank look on his face with just the trace of a smile, enough to irritate the other man but not provoke him.

"I had best be getting back to town," the head constable reached out to scratch behind the ass's ear. "You must be having a run of good luck, Clarke, acquiring a fine ass and cart like this."

Matthew ignored the snide remark, "Well I'll not keep you from your business. Good day to you Constable Armstrong," and he stepped inside Kitty Carroll's house, slamming the door behind him.

CHAPTER TWENTY-SIX

Matthew Clarke surveyed the landscaped garden around him, taking note of an elderly gardener working inside a greenhouse. He spotted William Harrington walking towards him across the neat lawn, carrying a jug and two glass tumblers.

"I thought you might like some water, its thirsty work digging a trench that size."

"I'm much obliged to you, Mr. Harrington, for the water and the work. I take it the old man yonder is a wee bit past his prime?"

"He is indeed Matthew. Johnson has been with my family since before I was born but these past few years have taken their toll on him, although he would be the last person to admit it. I caught the old boy trying to dig that ditch himself, too proud to ask for help."

"I'm thankful to whoever mentioned my name to you. You can rest assured the work will be done before the end of the day," Matthew drained his glass and handed it back. "I had best be getting on with it, Mr. Harrington."

"I'm told you are a man I can trust, is that so, Mr. Clarke," the solicitor's tone had become much more official.

"I like to think so. Who is it that's been singing my praises?"

"That's not important. In my business a man of your reputation is highly valued. The need to have that ditch built gave me the perfect opportunity to speak with you without arousing suspicion. I take it you are a good friend of James McGrother?"

"He was a good neighbour and a fellow fisherman. You don't sound like you are about to give me good news concerning him, Mr. Harrington," Matthew didn't like the way the conversation was going.

"It's in his own best interest that he stay in England. Constable Armstrong is like a dog with a bone when it comes to the McGrother name and he will not rest until he has James in jail. Do you think that Flannigan's demise has done your friend any favours?" asked Harrington.

"Are you asking me if I think it was an accident?"

"Do you not think he died under very suspicious circumstances? To be found with items on his person, that Pat McGrother had been accused of stealing months before, is a bit too much of a coincidence for my liking. However, I don't for one second believe that James McGrother had anything to do with Flannigan, or his death."

"Begging your pardon, sir, but I don't hold with speaking of things I know nothing about and I never put much store into local gossip. If you will excuse me now, I should be getting back to my work. As I said, I hope to have this ditch finished by the end of the day," Matthew swung his shovel over his shoulder.

"Yes, of course. I shouldn't be delaying you and I must be getting along myself. Call to the house when you have the work done and my wife will settle the account with you."

The smile left Matthew's face once his back was turned to the solicitor. In his head, he replayed the conversation he had just had and worried that he was being drawn into something that would have an adverse effect on either himself, or his son in America.

William Harrington, on the other hand, walked away from his house feeling more at ease having spoken with Matthew. For his own peace of mind, he had decided to approach the Blackrock fisherman directly and test out for himself the character of the man. The solicitor was not disappointed, what he had heard about Clarke had been true.

The head constable was not available when William called to the barracks, but the young policeman on duty was more than happy to be of help, answering every question that was put to him.

"So you were instructed by Constable Armstrong to go to the Democrat and give them the information about Flannigan's death, including the fact that some of the Devereux silverware was found on the body, is that so?"

"It is, Mr. Harrington. I thought it a bit premature, as the cause of death had not been officially established. But Constable Armstrong said that it was in the best interests of the case, with regards to the stolen goods, that is. He was most anxious that the papers have the information as soon as possible."

"I see," said Harrington, "I take it that it's normally the journalists who approach the police about such information, not the other way around."

"It is, sir, unless we are looking for someone or informing the public of something that they need to be aware of."

"Thank you, constable. You have been very helpful. Good day to you," the solicitor said.

William's next call was to the editor of the local newspaper, The Dundalk Democrat. Although he was satisfied with the information that the young constable had provided, he felt it would be wise to check out both sides of the story.

"I was very surprised at the police coming to *me* for a change. We usually find out about these things from local people first," the editor explained.

"You mean neighbours, fellow workers, hospital staff and the like?" asked Mr. Harrington.

"Yes, you know yourself how quickly word spreads in a community. Then we send a journalist to find out the facts but when it comes to obtaining information from the police – well, let's just say, it would be easier to get a priest to divulge what he hears in confession," laughed the editor.

"So it was most unusual, would you agree, for Constable Armstrong to send one of his men with information to a newspaper about a body that had just been discovered."

"It was, Mr. Harrington. That was why I specified in the paper that it *appeared* the man had broken his neck in a fall. We won't know that for definite until after the inquest but the two silver teaspoons found in his pocket were identified by Lord Devereux. Apparently, the head constable was adamant we print that in our report."

"Well, I won't take up any more of your time, Mr. Davis you have been most helpful."

As the solicitor left the building he was more determined than ever to convince James

McGrother that he must not return home, under any circumstances. If the inquest found that Flanagan had been murdered, it would not bode well for James. On the other hand, even if the death was declared to be an accident, Armstrong might still try to link the dead man to Pat McGrother and his nephew. The old fisherman and the thief were both dead and it would be easy to find someone in need of money to swear under oath that they had been seen together in the past. There would be no one to refute it and William Harrington was not sure to what lengths the head constable would go, in trying to make a case against James McGrother. That his uncle may have been acquainted with Flanagan was a possibility, as the elderly man may not even have known that he was in the company of a thief.

CHAPTER TWENTY-SEVEN

"I can save every spare farthing for the trip home, with three of you bringing a wage into the house that shouldn't be too difficult," said Mary.

"I don't want you taking that journey on your own and none of us can go with you. Even if I could take the time off work, both Maggie and Mr. Harrington have urged me not to return because of all the fuss being made over that Flanagan man," said James. "Besides, Peter was quite happy to have his youngest born here. This is our home now so I don't want to hear any more talk about you going back."

"If we lived in Liverpool, would you mind me going, it would only be half the distance?" asked Mary.

"Well we don't. Now let me get some sleep, woman, or I'll not be fit for work tomorrow," James turned his back to his wife, signalling the end of the discussion.

Mary lay stewing with frustration, knowing that sleep would not come easy while her mind continued to throw up ideas on how she would get back to Ireland for the birth of their next child. She calculated that there was another three months left before her baby would be born and she had already been saving the money for the trip.

"Two of your cousins live in Liverpool, James. Surely I could stay with one of them before setting off across the water. It would break up the journey."

James sighed and agreed to think about it over the weekend, when he had both the time and the energy to spare. It was enough to settle his wife's troubled mind and buy him a couple of day's peace before the discussion was taken up again.

By the time Sunday arrived Mary had summed up how much she would need for her trip. James had discreetly arranged for both his sisters-in-law to encourage her to remain in England for the baby's birth, but nothing that was said changed her thinking.

"Mary has a way of wearing a person down, doesn't she?" remarked Owen.

"She's a very determined woman. Once my wife sets her mind on something, she does it, there'll be no changing it. She doesn't know it yet, but I'm going to send Mary-Ann with her, for my own peace of mind. And wee Bridget has to go with them, sure there'll be nobody here to take care of her. I suppose the fresh air will do them all good."

"Rose is of the same opinion as yourself about the journey. She says that Mary has been quite ill of late and that it's not a good sign," said Owen, "She tells me that one of the doctors has said he will examine her if she goes up to the hospital."

"She won't go. Mary says having a child is as natural for a woman as breathing. She's happy to let Rose and her friend, the midwife, take care of her, but I have noticed she's looking thin of late. The baby seems to be growing fine, though," said James. "If she's faring any worse when the time comes, I'll put my foot down about the trip back over. Best not mention anything to young Mary-Ann about it, Owen. I don't want to get her hopes up just yet. She's missing home more than any of us and since we've been here, a week hasn't gone by that the poor wee mite isn't sickly."

"Don't fret over it, James. Maggie's youngest was in a worse state than your wee one and look at the lad now, fit as a fiddle," assured Owen.

As the weeks went by, Mary's health rapidly declined and it was in the middle of a wet, stormy night that Rose and James had to rush her to the hospital. He paced back and forth across the waiting room while his sister-in-law and the doctor on duty took care of his wife. An elderly woman gave him a sympathetic smile every time she caught his eye and appeared to be on the verge of speaking to him. James left the room to pace the corridor instead, he was not in the mood for conversation. When he saw Rose coming towards him he knew by her face that something was seriously wrong.

"Please, don't let it be Mary. If I have to lose one of them, please let it be the child," he silently prayed.

When she reached him, his sister-in-law linked his arm and led him back along the corridor, opening and closing doors until she found an empty room. By that stage James had already resigned himself to the fact that the news was not good but he was unable to find his voice to ask the question playing on his mind.

"Sit down, James. Mary is sleeping now, but she will need you when she wakes up. Can you stay here till then?" Rose waited for a response, continuing when James nodded his head. "Good. I must go home soon but I'll be back here for work later this morning. Owen will get word to your foreman that you are here, can you afford to lose a day's pay, James?"

The young man nodded his head, still afraid to ask about his wife and child. Instead, he looked up into Rose's eyes and waited for her to tell him the news.

"James, there is no easy way for you to hear this. Mary was carrying twins but she lost both of them, two little boys. It was much too early for them to come into the world, I'm so sorry. Neither myself nor the midwife had any notion that there were two babies, one must have been hiding behind the other. The doctor has given her something to make her sleep but when she wakes up he says it would be good if you were by her side. I'll leave you alone for a wee while and fetch us both a cup of tea."

"Twins you say, boys. Poor Mary, her heart will be broken. Does she know, Rose? Please don't say I have to tell her."

"She knows, James. That was why the doctor had to give her something, she was hysterical. Mary is weak but perfectly healthy, the doctor has assured me of that. She will probably be allowed home in a day or two, but she will need to take things easy for a while. Mary-Ann can look after her and wee Bridget until she's recovered. I'll be off now to get that tea."

CHAPTER TWENTY-EIGHT

"Can you believe that our Catherine will be sixteen next year? I feel ancient. Do you, James?"

"Mary, I have felt ancient ever since she was born. When children arrive youth goes out the window. Isn't that what you've always told me?" laughed James.

"Aye, it is, and speaking of children, I have some news for you," said Mary. "We are soon to have another one," she continued eating as if she had just made a remark about the weather.

James pushed his plate away and looked across the table. He had been enjoying the peace and quiet of a Sunday afternoon alone in the house with his wife, a rare occurrence. What he had eaten of the fine meal Mary had prepared for them began to feel like a lump of lead in his stomach.

"You don't look overly pleased about it, James."

"I'm not, Mary. Look what happened the last time you were with child, or should I say children?"

"Well, nothing is going to happen to this wee one. I'm going home, James, and don't try to stop me. I have been away long enough without even one visit back. Do you realize it has been more than three years since we laid eyes on your sister Maggie? I'll take Mary-Ann and Bridget with me. The air in Blackrock will do us all the power of good. Sure even the gentry take a trip there for the sea air and salt baths? We can stay with Maggie at Kitty Carroll's. Her daughter, Eliza is a good midwife, didn't she learned from the best? Between the three of them I will be treated like a queen and you can't get much safer than that."

Having recovered from the shock of hearing there would be an extra mouth to feed, James pulled his plate back towards him and began to eat once more.

"We may tell Mary-Ann tonight so, it will give her something to look forward to. When do you plan on going?" he asked, his mouth full.

"As soon as I can afford to. When do you think that may be?" asked Mary.

James took his time reckoning in his head what their savings amounted to. It didn't take too long, as he knew it wasn't very much.

"I suppose we could get the fare together over the next two months. Is that quick enough for you?"

Mary stood up to clear the table and spoke as she lifted their plates, "No, James, that will not be soon enough. I want to make sure this baby has the best chance I can give it, but I'm beginning to feel the same sickness I had the last time and I fear the air here is too thick for me to breathe. All I need is the fare until you are able to send over some money for our keep.

James stood behind Mary as she emptied some scraps into a bowl, for the hens they kept in their small back yard. Circling his arms around her soon-to-be expanded waistline, he nuzzled his face into the loose bun on the nape of her neck. Mary stopped moving and leaned back into him. They stood like statues, both of them savouring the moment. James was reminded of those times in the early days of their marriage, before the children came along.

Mary would have led him to their bed, teasing and tormenting him before finally melting into his arms, bringing them both to a place they had not been to in a long time. "Too long," thought James.

"I miss those early years, Mary. Don't you?" he whispered.

Mary tried to speak but her words just gathered in the back of her throat. Instead, she nodded her head, carefully lowering the plate she was holding. Turning around to kiss her husband's clean shaven face, she replied, "I miss your fisherman's beard, James. Don't you?"

"Sometimes, but it's far too hot in the foundry to be covering up my face with hair," he kissed her on the forehead and mentally rebuked himself for being so selfish in wanting to take her up to bed. He feared that Mary's condition was far too delicate and she would not want to risk harming the baby.

"I think I should go upstairs and lie down for a while, before the children arrive back from their picnic with Catherine. Will you come with me, James?" Mary had a glint in her eye.

"Are you teasing me now? Is that not too risky?" asked James.

"That is no more risk to the baby than when I haul your dirty work clothes to be washed and scrubbed every Saturday. Or do you have a mind to do your own laundry?" Mary laughed.

"Do you think Catherine is going to do it when you and Mary-Ann are across the water? I might as well start practicing now," he said.

"That girl doesn't even wash her own clothes, never mind yours. Well now, you will all just have to make do without me, won't you?" Mary was still in James's arms and poked him in the chest as she spoke.

"So, where you teasing me then?" James asked.

Mary twisted free from his embrace and was about to say something when the children burst noisily through the door.

"It was starting to look like rain, so we came back early," said Thomas, "And we're still hungry."

CHAPTER TWENTY-NINE

The grease that William Harrington rubbed into the rusted bolt on the old wooden gate, did its job. Sliding open the metal rod, the solicitor tugged at the handle but nothing moved. It had been many years since that entrance was last used and William had been hacking at the bushes all morning just to reach the overgrown gate. He knew the only way to get it open would be to push from the other side, so he quickly made his way across the lawn and onto the street at the front of the house.

As he walked around to the back of his garden, which entailed climbing over a fence, the solicitor made sure that there was nobody about. Satisfied that there were no onlookers, William proceeded to attack the overgrown shrubbery and nettles that covered the high, stone wall. Swinging a small scythe to and fro, it wasn't long before he had made a clearing to the arched gateway. A few good kicks and the wooden gate swung open, taking the solicitor by surprise. He fell headlong into his back garden, watched by a herd of curious cattle whose grazing he had interrupted.

That evening after dinner, Mrs. Harrington informed her husband that she would be calling on a neighbour across the street.

"That was very observant of you, William, noticing how lonely Mrs. Ashton seems to be of late. Of course, she would never admit to it, she's a very proud lady, but she did tell me how much she would be looking forward to my visit this evening. I hope you don't mind me leaving you here on your own, the house is very quiet once the children are asleep. Or would you care to accompany me?"

The solicitor declined and assured his wife that he had a lot of work to catch up on and that she should have a nice long visit with the lonely old widow. As soon as he was left alone, William Harrington made his way to the bottom of his large garden. While he waited, with his eyes fixed on the old gate, he listened for some sort of signal that he presumed would be used. There was no moon to light up the sky and only a few stars managed to shine their way through the thick clouds.

After what seemed an age, a hand flew out from behind William and fixed itself firmly across his mouth. He felt a sharp pointed object dig into his back through his lightly padded lounge jacket. Before he even had time to panic, a shadow came from his left and the dark form of a tall, broad man stood in front of him.

"I'm sorry to be so furtive, Mr. Harrington, but I'm sure you understand my reasons," a low, mellow voice sounded through the darkness.

As the hand was withdrawn from his mouth, William wiped his lips with his sleeve and whispered that he was fully aware of the need for discretion, for both their sakes.

"Do you have a trustworthy man who would be willing to work here as an assistant gardener? It would be the best way for us to communicate. I can afford to pay him for three days labour each week. My own man is getting along in years so it would not look suspicious were he to have a helper. In fact, I have been telling him he needs an assistant these past six months."

"I know the very man and I think you have already given him a trial, have you not?" said the voice.

"I had a feeling it would be Clarke, so it was you who sent his name to me. If you are happy to trust him, then so am I," said William. "I have a favour to ask of you concerning James McGrother, may I be so bold as to speak of it?"

There was a moment's awkward silence. "I'm not in a position to risk any more involvement in that business, if you know what I mean, Mr. Harrington. I don't think I can be of any further assistance to your client."

"Please, sir, hear me out. I'll not trouble you again with this, if you are absolutely sure that it is beyond your capabilities."

The mellow voice told William to carry on but that time was running out and they would need to bring their meeting to a close very soon.

"James McGrother gave me the proceeds from the sale of his boat, with instructions to hand it over to Lord Devereux. He hoped it would clear his family's name. You don't believe they had anything to do with those stolen goods found on Flanagan, do you?" asked the solicitor.

"I know for a certainty they didn't. That lying thief received his just desserts, I would say," the voice laughed softly.

"Constable Armstrong is still convinced that Pat McGrother and his nephew had a hand in the theft of that silverware. He was in great haste to make sure the Democrat printed the story of Flanagan's death, then he had a paper delivered anonymously to the McGrother house in England. That tells me one thing – the head constable is trying to lure James back to Ireland to trap him in some way. He might very well use the evidence of a false witness in order to arrest him and throw him in jail," the solicitor waited for a response.

"What do you think we can do about that? Kidnap McGrother for his own safety?"

"No, no, you misunderstand. I know of three people, two men and a woman, that would be willing to perjure themselves for a nice sum of money from Armstrong. He has done this before but I cannot prove it," William produced a piece of folded paper. "Here are their details. Please, take it. If you can find a way to put pressure on these people I would be eternally grateful. Others who might be tempted will then think twice about getting involved. You know that I have certain political contacts but they cannot be associated with the case, otherwise I would have asked for their help before now."

"Yet you assume that we are willing to take that risk?" the voice sounded sharp to William.

"We are all on the same side, regardless of class or religion, sir. I feel that a further miscarriage of justice may be avoided if something can be done to warn off those people. For my part, I have made arrangements to secure a promotion for Armstrong, thus ensuring his relocation. It will take some months and I fear that every week that goes by poses a threat to James McGrother's freedom. I do not think he realizes how close he is to being arrested and I cannot tell him what I know."

"I will see what can be done Mr. Harrington, but I make no promises," the mellow voice said, as its owner took the paper from William's hand. "Clarke will receive word about his new position with your staff. It will be up to you to pay him enough to ensure that he comes here every week, after all he has a family to provide for. Now, I have delayed long enough. We will take our leave of you, Mr. Harrington. Goodnight, sir."

The two bulky shadows moved away from William and disappeared through the arched gateway. Left alone at the end of his garden the solicitor listened carefully for voices or movement outside of his boundary walls. Only the sounds of the night could be heard, amplified in the still air – a dog barking in the distance and the flapping of wings overhead, possibly an owl on the hunt. Satisfied that the men had gotten safely away, William bolted the gate before crossing his neat lawn and entering the French doors to his dining room. Once inside, he realized how much he had perspired as he wiped beads of sweat from his forehead.

Making his way through the dark house, the solicitor was thankful his wife had not yet returned and that the only live-in members of staff were Johnson, the gardener, and an equally old butler. As he walked across the parts of the floor devoid of carpet, William's footsteps echoed through the quiet house. Undisturbed, the two elderly men remained asleep in their basement quarters, and the children were in the same state upstairs.

When Mrs. Harrington walked briskly into the drawing room she found her husband sitting by the fire, his eyes closed and a book on his lap. She felt it was a shame to wake him, but the hour was late and they would be retiring for the night shortly. The news she had been about to share with him would have to wait until morning. Knowing he would lie awake thinking on it for half the night, tossing and turning, Mrs. Harrington had no intention of losing a night's sleep over one of her husband's charity cases.

CHAPTER THIRTY

As she had predicted, Mrs. Harrington's husband worried all through breakfast about the implications Lord Devereux's death might have on the McGrother case. The solicitor was only too happy, for once, that their gossipy neighbour had informed his wife of the event the night before.

"I daresay she knew of his passing before he was even aware of it himself," he laughed.

"Now, now, William, no need for such sarcasm. Mrs. Ashton and her inquisitive nature can be very useful at times. You know how much you hate being taken by surprise. At least this morning you will be well prepared for all those eager bearers of bad news and you can thank our nosey neighbour for that."

"Indeed I can. In fact, it will be me spreading the gossip for a change. I doubt many will have heard of the old boy's demise yet, although by mid-morning even the dogs in the street will be aware of it, I daresay."

"Yes, well, be that as it may, I had better get ready for my meeting with the ladies. We will have to organize a visit on behalf of the committee to pay our condolences to the family," she kissed her husband on the forehead. "I'm not sure I can meet you for lunch today as planned, William."

The solicitor assured his wife that his own day may not go according to plan, either, "I shall see you this evening, my dear," he said. "Give my regards to the ladies."

There were few people taken by surprise at the news William brought to work with him that day. Although he arrived earlier than usual at his office, the word about Lord Devereux's passing was already spread around the town. Not handing over James McGrother's money had been a sound decision, and the solicitor congratulated himself at having the foresight to delay taking that step. He knew that the estate was in debt and even if Pat McGrother's name was cleared, it would be very difficult to get the money back. With the passing of the old Lord, there would be no chance of recovering anything owed to the McGrother family.

In a much more positive frame of mind, William called his clerk into the office. He was about to draft a letter to be sent to James and for once it would be good news, in spite of the fact that he would be reminding his client that it was in his best interest to remain in England.

******

Mary could not believe her ears when the letter from Mr. Harrington was read out to her. She made James go over it one more time.

"Bless his heart, do you realize what this means, James? We can all go home now. Isn't that grand?" Mary looked around the table at her family.

Catherine and Thomas looked at each other with scowls on their faces and James kept his eyes on the headed notepaper in his hand.

"We have work here, Ma. What good would it do to go home? Sure all the money would be gone in no time," said Thomas.

"I'm not going, ye can all go without me. I'll stay with Owen and Rose or maybe I could be a live-in domestic," argued Catherine. "That's it, I'll live-in."

"You'll do no such thing, you're barely fifteen, do you think I'm leaving you here on your own?" scolded Mary.

James told the children to go to bed and they could talk about it next day, after Mass, when the news had sunk in properly. Once they had the parlour to themselves, Mary continued to speak about the whole family moving back to Ireland.

"I know how much it would mean to you, love, but Mr. Harrington warned me in the letter not to think about going back, at least not for the present. And Thomas is correct in saying the money wouldn't last too long if we gave up the work we have here. It's good to know that we have some savings in Ireland and in time it will make it easier for us to settle back home, but for now, Mary, I think it best we carry on as we had intended. I will keep an eye on Catherine and Thomas."

"I suppose what you say makes sense, James. I wouldn't want Armstrong to get his evil hands on you again. Oh why is it that good news always comes with a sacrifice? I don't ask for much, do I? Is going home with my family too much to hope for?"

James held onto his wife and consoled her, knowing it was her condition that was making her feel so dismal.

"It's the fragile state you're in that has you so morose. You were looking forward to seeing Maggie and all the neighbours, that hasn't changed has it?" he asked.

"No, I still want to see them, but when you read out what the letter said about the money it got my hopes up. Now I feel like the wind's been taken out of my sails."

"It won't be for ever, Mary. Didn't I promise you that someday we would all be home again?"

"That was after I lost the twins, James. I thought you were saying it to make me feel better, you seem to have settled here much easier than I expected you to," said Mary. "Anyways, neither of us are very good at keeping our promises, are we?"

"Ah Mary, don't talk like that or you'll drag me down with you. If I'm to be truthful, you are sickening for home more than I ever thought you would."

There was a movement on the stairs and Mary called out to whoever was lurking behind the curtain. Catherine stepped into the room, a look of defiance across her young face.

"I had to make sure ye were not planning on taking me back with ye. Da is talking sense and you need to listen to him, Ma."

"It's bad manners to eavesdrop on other people's conversations. Did we not teach you anything? I hope that's not the way you behave at the doctor's house," snapped Mary.

James had gone to stand beside his daughter, "Your Ma is right, Catherine. You shouldn't have been hiding behind the curtain like that. If you want to know something, ask us to our faces."

"Da, I already know the answer. You would be gone back to Ireland, quick as a flash, if it weren't for that constable that hates your guts and if Ma goes over I doubt she'll ever return. Now, do *you* have any questions for *me* – like, where do *I* want to live? Or do either of you care?"

Catherine's head was yanked sideways as her mother pulled her by her long braided hair, causing her to lose her balance and stumble towards the fireplace. As the girl's hand came down onto the hot, iron stove, the sound of skin sizzling was drowned out by her scream. James grabbed hold of his daughter, steering her through the front door and down the street, towards the communal pump, leaving Mary's apologetic cries behind them.

"Keep it under the water for a few minutes. The pain will lessen after a while," James pumped the handle until the water flowed.

"It hurts, Da. I've never had a burn this bad. Will I be able to work, it's my good hand?"

James rolled up his sleeves and held out both his arms, turning them slowly. There were scars randomly scattered along the length of his limbs. Catherine had never really paid much heed to them before.

"Try working in the foundry for a week, love. You soon get used to the burns and scalds."

"Do you hate working there? Is that why you want to go back to Ireland?" asked Catherine.

James pulled down his sleeves and examined the hot, red patch on his daughter's right palm.

"I'm not like my brothers, Catherine, they would never return home. I think your Aunt Maggie understands me even more than your mother does. That's why I wasn't surprised when she refused to come with us, I know how she feels about leaving Ireland. I hope with all my heart that one day your mother and myself will live once again in our old parish and that I

179

will still have the strength to fish on a boat in the bay. As for you and your brother and sisters, I think it will be a long time before you have to decide on where you will live, so let's not worry too much about it for now. Are we agreed?"

Catherine nodded her head and let her father wrap his arm around her to lead her back to the house. Mary could not look either of them in the eye when they came through the door. She had been tearing up some strips from an old, well boiled sheet to make a bandage for her daughter's burned palm.

"Let me bind this around your hand, my love. We can show it to Rose in the morning. Oh Catherine, I'm so sorry, I never meant to hurt you."

James left them both alone, making an excuse to go up to bed early. Catherine looked at her mother, who was a little smaller in height than herself, and told her she wasn't bearing any grudges against her for the burn.

"It was an accident, Ma. I tripped. It doesn't hurt so much now, the cold water took the sting out of it. Da says we should stop fussing about going home for now and wait till the time comes, before worrying over what should be done. But I won't change my mind about it. I work long, hard days but I'm treated kindly and fed well, and if I play my cards right, I might even become a lady's maid. Do you see why I can't go home with ye, Ma?"

Mary nodded as she finished wrapping the cloth around Catherine's hand. She looked at her almost grown up daughter and smiled. "I forget that you're nearly a woman, love, with your own dreams and plans. Your Da is right, we should not be arguing over decisions that don't need to be made yet. Go on up to bed now, or you'll be falling asleep in Mass tomorrow."

The sound of a hacking cough from the children's bedroom overhead drew their attention to the ceiling. As they both looked up, footsteps could be heard crossing the creaky wooden floors.

"Your Da's gone in to her, she'll be alright after a good cough and a pat on the back," said Mary sounding a lot less worried than she actually was.

"Poor Mary-Ann, I'm glad she's going with you, Ma. She needs the fresh air to help her get better."

Catherine knew that it was only a matter of time before her father would also be ready to return to his roots. She resolved in her heart there and then, not to allow him talk her into going back. She knew that Thomas would be allowed to stay, because he was a boy and in an apprenticeship that would be impossible to keep up once back in Ireland. Catherine's only chance was if she could get out of the kitchen, where most of her work took place. She felt sure her mother would agree to her staying in England if she had a better position in the doctor's household.

CHAPTER THIRTY-ONE

The words on the letter blurred as James tried to focus through weary eyes. It was his third time reading the neat script of Haggardstown's parish priest. Mary had asked him to write on her behalf, letting the family in England know that her son was born in good health and both of them were thriving.

"Are you crying, Da," asked Thomas, concerned.

"Not at all, son. I'm just tired from work and from reading in this dim light. Can I stop going over it now, Catherine? That's the third time you've heard it."

"If you would let me have the letter I could read it for myself, or Thomas could. He's a better reader than either of us."

"That's not fair. Da is good at the reading, aren't you, Da?" said the boy in his father's defence.

"Off to bed with ye both, there's personal things in this letter from your Ma to me," James herded them out of the parlour. "Give me a bit of peace before I sleep, will ye?"

"What sort of thing would Ma get a priest to write that we couldn't read?" teased Catherine.

Listening to his eldest children laughing as they ascended the stairs, James said a quick prayer of thanks that all had gone well with the birth and that it had been a boy. It might help to ease the hurt that Mary still felt at the loss of her twin sons.

There was a light rap at the window and James looked up to see his brother's face smiling in at him.

"I see you're managing to keep up with your washing," Owen remarked, pointing to the clothes hanging over the stove. "I heard you got a letter, is it about Mary? Did she have the baby, yet?"

"Rose sent you up, didn't she?" laughed James. "She must have been itching to know what was in it, ever since she took delivery of it from the postman this morning."

"She told me she left it on the mantelpiece so you would see it as soon as you came home," said Owen.

James was very grateful to his sister-in-law, who made a meal for them on the mornings she was off work, leaving it on the back of the warm stove to cook slowly through the day.

"I'm much obliged to Rose for looking after us the way she does. I don't thank her enough."

"She knows you appreciate it, James. Now, are you going to tell me your news or will you let me go back to my wife empty-handed, to get beaten over the head?"

James laughed and gave his brother the good news about Mary and the baby. Owen produced a bottle from his pocket and pointed to the cups hanging on hooks nearby.

"I came prepared to wet a baby's head," he said. "We'll tell the rest of the family in the morning but for now let's just the two of us drink to your new wee son," the men tapped their cups off each other.

"I have some news for you myself, James, but I warn you it's not good. Were you aware that Flanagan was collecting money in Liverpool and Manchester for the Fenians?"

"Aye, sure that's a well-known fact. What has it to do with me?" asked James.

"Wasn't his body found with the silverware on it that Uncle Pat was supposed to have stolen?"

"It was and isn't that a good thing? Although Mr. Harrington doesn't seem to think it will do me any favours. Constable Armstrong is convinced that I was involved with that no good thief," James's mood had darkened.

Owen checked behind the curtain, making sure the children were not within earshot. "I was told by a reliable source that Armstrong is trying to link you to the Fenians," he whispered.

"How can he do that? Sure I've never even attended one of their fund raisings, not even when they were held in Paddy Mac's. Who gave you that information?" asked James.

Owen was very quiet and hesitated, not sure how he should answer his brother's question.

"Tell me you're not a Fenian. It's one thing to be a sympathizer, it's another to be a member. You haven't done anything that could bring trouble upon us, have you Owen?"

"Have you had any news from Michael and Brigid Kiernan lately?"

"From America? The last letter we got was a good six months ago," James stared at his brother.

It slowly dawned on James what Owen was trying to tell him. Michael was involved with the Fenian movement.

"James, I know there's not much support at the moment in Ireland, it's early days yet. But outside of the country, especially in America, it's growing fast. There's a lot of young men, and women too by all accounts, who feel that they were forced into exile."

"I'm not surprised that Michael is involved. Was it him that got word to you about Armstrong? Did he ask you to warn me, Owen?" James knew the answer before his brother had the chance to nod his head.

"You didn't answer my question. Please tell me neither yourself nor Peter are Fenians. Is there no peace to be had in this life for me?" James was raising his voice.

"Hush, now. You'll wake the children. None of us nor our sons have had anything to do with them. We are all far too busy keeping a roof over our heads and food on the table, to have the time or inclination. But I had to make sure that you haven't been involved yourself, on account of your friend, Michael. He sent word to me about warning you not to return to Ireland, not even for a funeral, at least not until Armstrong has been moved on."

"That could be years yet, he's not been that long in Dundalk," said James.

"Ah sure, the police are never stationed for too many years in the one town. Anyway, I get the feeling something is afoot to speed up his departure. But you cannot ignore two warnings – one from a solicitor and one from a Fenian, can you James?"

The younger brother shook his head, "You had better be getting back to Rose with the news about the baby. It's a wonder she hasn't been knocking on the door already," a thought struck James, "She knew you would be asking me about other matters, is that not so?

"She's the one who got the news from Brigid. Michael Kiernan is a clever man, he knows it's far less suspicious for women to send and receive such messages. I'll leave you be, James, you have a lot to think about. I doubt you will get much sleep tonight."

******

Mary watched her baby's even breathing and noted how like James he was. It made her heart ache for the other half of her family across the water, the sound of the sea in the still night air reminding her of the distance between them. What Maggie had told her played on Mary's mind and prevented her from joining her son in slumber. She wished she could have seen her husband's face when he received the news that he had a son. Thomas would be pleased to at last have a brother, even though he was a long time in coming. Catherine would worry that she would have another sibling to mind, but love him just the same.

Those thoughts ran through Mary's head alongside one that she feared might never happen, the hope of bringing her family back home. As Catherine and Thomas grew older, the likelier they were to stay put. They had regular work in establishments that treated them well and had formed friendships with their neighbours' children, but they were still so young. Mary was not ready to part from them and she knew in her heart that James wasn't either. However, there was one member of the family that caused her the most concern.

Mary-Ann had thrived in the few weeks that she was back in Blackrock, and Mary knew it was due to more than the excitement of the visit home and the arrival of a little brother. The racking cough had all but disappeared and her sleep at night was no longer broken. She had even put on weight and a rosy glow had returned to her cheeks, causing everyone to remark on how well she was looking. As Mary drifted off to sleep her mind was already preparing her heart for a decision that had to be made soon.

"He's a hungry one, you'll need to eat well to satisfy him, Mary," Maggie laughed at breakfast next morning.

"A meal like this one will certainly help, you still make the best bread in the parish," Mary said. "Look at him. Isn't he the spit of his father? I wish James were here now to see him."

Maggie leaned in close to examine the baby's face, "It's like looking into my brother's eyes and that's for sure. Are you going to call him Jamie or James?"

"You're his godmother, you decide."

"I suppose you should call him Jamie. At least that way when you let a roar at your husband, your son won't think it's him that's in trouble. Sure they'll all call him wee Jamie anyway, over yonder, like we did with Owen's youngest. I take it you'll be going back, Mary."

"I had a mind to stay, Maggie. Look how well Mary-Ann is since we got here. How can I watch her sicken again?" Mary could see her two youngest daughters playing just outside the open door. "She loves you as much as she loves me, did you know that?"

"Sure Mary-Ann loves everyone, she's that sort of child," remarked Maggie.

"I know what needs to be done, and I hope you'll agree with me. James cannot come back here, not for now anyway, and I wouldn't want to put him in any danger from that lunatic, Armstrong. If yourself and the Carrolls would be in agreement, I would like to leave Mary-Ann in your care over the winter months. I'll make sure you receive payment towards her keep. What do you say?"

"Oh Mary, there's nothing I would like more and you don't have to worry about the money. I'm managing fine on the work the hotel gives me in the busy months, I even have enough left over to see me through the winter. If I need it I'll ask, sure I wouldn't see the poor wee mite go hungry, would I?"

"I'll still be sending you something, Maggie, so let's not argue about it. I must pay Mr. Harrington one last visit before I leave. Do you think I could travel into town with the Clarkes on their next trip?"

"Of course, Mary. You can leave the girls here with me. Why don't we call on Lizzie now, while it's still early? I have a feeling tomorrow is one of the days that Matthew works on Mr. Harrington's garden. You could maybe go in with him and pay a visit to the lady of the house while you're there," laughed Maggie. "Although by all accounts, she's an uppity one, not a bit like her husband. He's a grand man, for a Protestant, isn't he?"

CHAPTER THIRTY-TWO

At the end of a long and tiring Sunday, James and Mary lay in bed watching their youngest son, well fed and fast sleep in his mother's arms. There had been a stream of visitors to the house all day, calling to see the latest arrival to the street. Mary was exhausted, having arrived the day before after a long journey, with a baby and young child to care for.

"He's a hungry one, it'll take all I can earn to feed this one, that's for sure," James stroked his son's rosy cheek.

"Have you forgiven me for leaving Mary-Ann behind?"

"There's nothing to forgive, Mary, but I wish you had let me know of your plans. It was a shock when I saw you standing at the station and no sign of her anywhere."

"I'm sorry for that, James. I didn't think it through, I was afraid I might change my mind. As soon as I had made the decision I called to Mr. Harrington and got the price of the fare from him. That was when he said we should put the money into that new bank that opened in Ardee. He said he was afraid we would lose it should something happen to him. I hope he's not ailing, James, he's a good man."

"It was the best thing to do with it. We won't touch it unless we are starving or in danger of being evicted. Let's just forget we have it, Mary, that way it will be there for us when we return home."

"So you agree that we should move back, do you?"

"But not until Catherine and Thomas are old enough to leave behind. We'll send Maggie some money for Mary-Ann's keep and save what we can from what's left."

Mary put the sleeping baby into the cradle that had been passed through the family. She curled up inside the embrace of her husband's arms and sighed contentedly, happy to be back in the one place that gave her a sense of permanence and security. Just before sleep overtook them, Mary whispered to James that together they could face anything life threw at them. "We can, love," he replied.

Next morning a letter was handed to James by a young boy who told them he didn't know the man who had paid him to deliver it. After being given a description of the stranger, neither James nor Mary had any idea who it could have been.

"Well, open it, James. It could be from Mr. Harrington."

As his eyes quickly ran along the neatly written script, James expression changed from confusion to concern and as soon as he had finished reading it he rolled the letter into a ball and threw it into the hot stove.

"James, what kind of news could make you do such a thing," Mary exclaimed.

"Nothing that should be repeated. Forget that we ever received that letter. Don't tell a soul about it, do you hear me?"

Mary knew by the paleness of her husband's face that something was very wrong, "I promise I won't breathe a word of it to anyone, but you have to tell me what it was about, James. Who sent the cursed letter? Was it Mr. Harrington?"

"It was from America, from Michael," James whispered as if the whole street was listening outside their door.

"Michael who?" asked Catherine as she came into the parlour rubbing her eyes.

"Oh we were just talking about a man I work with. Here, eat your breakfast up or we'll be late," James shot Mary a warning glance, "I'll go up and make sure Thomas is awake before we go."

It wasn't until late in the evening, when the children were in bed, that the discussion of the letter was taken up again. James had been grateful for the long hours at work to think on how much he should disclose to his wife. She would know by its furtive delivery, that there was more to the letter than greetings from America, and a bit of gossip about the friends they had in common who had moved there. James would have to come up with a plausible enough reason for why Michael had not sent news through the postal system, as he usually did.

"Well, are you going to give me the news from Michael, or do you think I can read your mind, James?" Mary stroked her baby's soft hair as he fed.

"Michael and Brigid and the children are fine, and send their love. Matthew Clarke's son, Daniel, and his friend, John McDermott are lodging in their house. Isn't that grand, Mary?"

"We already knew that, sure didn't I bring that news back with me from Maggie? What was it that made you burn the letter, James? You're being as secretive as a Fenian."

"Hush, woman. Be careful what you say, that's nothing to be loose-lipped about," hissed James.

"Are you involved with the Fenians?" Mary ignored the warning.

James stood up abruptly and the noise of his chair scraping loudly on the floor startled the sleeping baby. Mary rocked him in her arms as she watched her husband peer through the window into the dimly lit street.

"By all that's holy, have you no sense. Please stop asking me questions like that," he whispered.

"James, I don't care if Michael Kiernan is a Fenian. In fact, it wouldn't surprise me at all, but look me in the eye and swear to me on Pat's grave that you are not involved yourself."

"Mary, on my uncle's grave and on Annie's too, I swear that I've had nothing to do with any political organization. Nor have my brothers, I'm sure of it. But there is one person I've had my suspicions about and after reading that letter from Michael, I'm more convinced than ever I was right."

James went very quiet and continued to watch the street. His silence frustrated Mary to a point where she felt the urge to hit him over the head with a pan, until a thought struck her.

"Is it Maggie?" she whispered.

Turning to face her, James nodded his head, "Michael wrote that he is coming to England next month and would like to meet up with me. When he finishes whatever business he has here, he will be travelling to Ireland before his return to America. He offered to deliver any news I might have to my sister. He said he will be staying in The Blackrock Hotel, and joked that she may very well be the one who empties his chamber pot."

"He still has a sense of humour, I'll give him that. Remember when he was here, lodging with Maggie, how she used to curse him and the boys for leaving their bucket fill to the brim before emptying it," smiled Mary.

"If Maggie is involved with the Fenians, there is a good chance that Armstrong will find out – and you've left Mary-Ann with her," said James.

Realizing the implications of what her husband was saying, Mary tried to control a feeling of panic that was beginning to rise. If anything was to happen to Maggie, their daughter would be taken away by the police. With no immediate family left to care for her, it would be the perfect excuse for Armstrong to inflict even more suffering on the McGrothers.

"Surely your sister has more sense than that, James. Didn't the Church threaten to excommunicate anyone who joined the Fenians?"

The previous year an Irish Cardinal had refused to allow a Dublin cathedral service to a former rebel, Thomas Bellew McManus, who had died in America. He had been given a state-like funeral by New York's Irish exiles when his remains were taken to Saint Patrick's Cathedral on 5th Avenue, before he was brought back to Ireland. In spite of Cardinal Cullen's refusal to allow McManus's coffin into any of the Dublin churches, some thirty thousand mourners attended his funeral at Glasnevin cemetery.

"Such a threat would only serve to make my sister more determined, you know yourself she's as stubborn as a mule. Mary, I'm going to meet up with Michael when he gets to Liverpool, he's speaking at a gathering there and has given me a password to use if I want to arrange a meeting with him. I'll ask him to talk Maggie into coming back here with Mary-Ann. If she thinks it will help the Fenian cause, I daresay she will be happy to oblige. Can you think of any other way to get them over?"

Mary was quiet for a few moments as she walked around the kitchen table, rocking the sleeping baby.

"Oh James, I can't. I pray that your plan works. I'll be like a bag of cats until I have my child safely back with us."

CHAPTER THIRTY-THREE

Through the grimy glass of an upstairs window Michael Kiernan scanned the surrounding rooftops. He was in the back bedroom of a small house on a narrow street. One particular roof caught his eye and Michael's lips curled into a sly smile. It was the one that belonged to the Bridewell on Argyle Street, and his men had not been amused when they learned how close the police would be to the-ir lodgings. When Michael convinced them that the safest place to be was right under the constables' noses, they eventually saw the funny side of it.

Listening to the various noises coming from the backstreet below, Michael reflected on how much his life had changed since the last time he had been in Liverpool. Although it seemed a lifetime ago, he could remember every detail clearly, as if it had been only a week before. A few sharp knocks on wood jolted him out of his memories and Michael unlocked the paint-chipped door. In the hallway stood his old friend, James McGrother. The men stared at each other for all of five seconds, before Michael took hold of the lapels of his visitor's jacket and dragged him into the room. They clasped hands and shook them vigorously.

"Did you like the password I sent you, James?"

"It was an easy one to remember. What made you think of 'seashells'? Our fishing days?"

Michael took a string of small shells from his pocket and asked, "Do you recognize these? You

195

gave them to me before I left for America. I carry them everywhere, they're my lucky charms."

"Michael, you haven't changed a bit," said James as he warmly embraced his friend.

"I can't say the same for you. Are you wearing every stitch you possess, or have you put on some weight at last."

"I've managed to improve my diet, work has been good these past few years. What about yourself and Brigid, and Francis and all your wee ones. How many do ye have now?"

Michael smiled and replied that Francis was almost a man and as tall as himself. Then he listed the names of five more children. "One died not long after his birth. I nearly lost Brigid, too. What about your own brood? And Mary, how is she? Well, I hope."

James told his friend about the loss of his twin sons and the healthy arrival of the latest one. He spoke of how well Catherine and Thomas were doing in their jobs, and the way his youngest daughter, Brigid, could melt a heart of stone, but his voice changed when he mentioned Mary-Ann.

"I need a favour from you, Michael, but first you must answer a question as honestly as you can," James paused as a knock sounded on the door.

Michael opened it and stepped briefly into the hallway, then returned carrying a tray of tea, sandwiches, a decanter of whiskey and two glasses.

"This, my friend, is none other than *Malcolm Brown's* whiskey, all the way from his distillery in Dundalk. It brings to mind the time we robbed a half a jug from Paddy Mac's. What were we? Eight, nine?" laughed Michael.

"I think we were only seven, it was on one of my visits to Blackrock. Do you recall how my brothers would leave me with Pat and Annie for the summer months? As I got older and left school I stayed at home in Monaghan working the bogs and fields, so I don't think we were much past the age of eight."

"Even worse," laughed Michael, "Drunken seven year olds found lying in their own vomit in Peter Matthew's boat, tangled in his nets. Do you remember the beating we got from my father when we were carried home and dumped on his doorstep? And the sore heads next day?"

"I do. You got off lightly, I got another thrashing from Annie when I was fit enough to stand. I'm not sure which end of me hurt the most," James recalled.

"I sent one of the men out to find me some *Malcolm Brown* for this evening, in your honour James. I knew it was sold in Liverpool, sure the half of county Louth is over here working and that's the truth, isn't it?" Michael raised his glass to examine the golden liquid.

"I'm not sure I want to be reminded of a thrashing I received when I was eight, but I'm much obliged for the thought," James took a mouthful from his own glass and saluted Michael, "And for the drink, of course."

When the two men had finished reminiscing, their conversation took on a more serious nature and Michael asked his friend about the favour he had mentioned earlier.

"Is my sister Maggie O'Neill a member of the Irish Republican Brotherhood?" asked James.

197

"Why must you be so formal? You sound like a barrister. Call her a Fenian. Is that not what everyone else says?"

"So you admit that she is?"

Michael took another sip of his whiskey before answering the question.

"No, James. I admit to nothing and that's the way it has to be in the Brotherhood. She might be involved in some way, but only those belonging to the circle operating in her area would know that for sure. Maggie is more than likely a sympathizer but not a member. Are you afraid for her safety, James?"

"One of our daughters, Mary-Ann, is a sickly child and Mary left her in Blackrock with Maggie to build up her strength. I've been having problems with the head constable in Dundalk these past few years. But something tells me you are already aware of that, Michael. Anyway, he would only love to find a reason to interfere with my family. I'm afraid Maggie might give him one, not intentionally of course, but Armstrong is a sly man and misses nothing."

"What do you think I can do about it, James, short of kidnapping your sister and dragging her back with me?" asked Michael.

"All I ask it that you convince her of the need to support the cause here in England, in Sunderland, that is if you think she is involved in the first place. If Maggie has had anything to do with the Fenians, then she will feel duty bound to act on what you have to say. On no account mention the fact that I'm worried about Armstrong arresting her, she has no fear and would defy him to the last if she thought it would irritate him. Will you do it, Michael? For the sake of my sister and my daughter."

Michael held out a hand to James and as they shook on it he said, "Don't worry, I'll find a way of convincing Maggie that she is needed in Sunderland and I will pay her passage over and that of your daughter's."

"No need to pay, I have the fare here," James pulled a small bag from his pocket.

"I'll bring the money with me, if it makes you feel better. You're as stubborn as your sister so I'll not waste my breath arguing with you. Can you stay here with me tonight, James? We can have supper together and finish this decanter of whiskey."

"I'm sorry Michael, I've already lost a day's wage. Isn't it a grand thing to be able to travel across the country in a railway carriage and be back home in my own bed by midnight?"

"Aye, it is indeed. Not like when we first came here and had to work our way across on a barge. I'll never forget the fright you gave me when you took sick," said Michael.

"There's no fear of that this time. Well, I'll be saying goodbye to you so," James held his arms open wide and smiled sadly at his friend.

The two men embraced, wishing each other safe journeys and good lives, then Michael unlocked the door. Listening to the sound of his friend's footsteps echo down the hallway, he was relieved that he had chosen to sleep in the room at the back of the house. If he had been standing at that moment in the front bedroom, he may have been tempted to watch as James left the street. It would have been too painful for him to see another person he loved walk out of

199

his life. Michael was thankful that he had kept his true circumstances to himself. Glad that he had not told James how Brigid had thrown him out of the house, when she found out he was involved with the Brotherhood, and that he had not laid eyes on his children in over six months.

CHAPTER THIRTY-FOUR

A knowing smile crept over James's face as he listened to his sister tell the family, who were gathered around her, how much she had missed them all. Maggie's return to England had answered his question about her political activities and he would be forever grateful to Michael for the part he played in her return. James listened with amusement as Maggie recounted tales of sleepless nights spent worrying over her family in England and that, much as she loved the land of her birth, she had come to realize that her place was with her flesh and blood.

"That's not the impression I got when I was over there, Rose," whispered Mary.

"Maybe when you left it gave her a longing to follow you over. Mind you, it seems strange that she didn't wait until the winter was behind us, for young Mary-Ann's sake," replied Rose.

Mary inched her way past the captive audience until she was standing next to her husband. She slipped her hand into his and led him towards the front door. There was a chill in the air and Mary took a coat from a hook on the wall to wrap around her shoulders.

"Can we take a wee walk down the street, James?"

"What is it you want to ask me, Mary?" was his reply as he fell into step beside her.

"Is that the only time I pay any heed to you, when I have a question for you? Maybe I just want to spend some time alone with my husband" Mary replied.

James laughed and put an arm around her shoulders.

"But I'm right, aren't I? You have something to ask me."

"James McGrother, there's times when I could strangle you. I've half a mind to go back to the house," Mary had stopped walking.

"Mary McGrother, there's nothing half-minded about you. Now tell me, what it is you want to know. I'll be relieved if the word *baby* is not in the next sentence you say to me."

There was a burst of laughter from Mary, "It might be," she smiled. "Wouldn't it be grand for wee Jamie to have a brother to play with?"

"Tell me you're teasing me, Mary. That's not something to jest about," James was beginning to perspire and it wasn't from the walk.

"That's true, I shouldn't tempt fate like that," Mary looked around, making sure there were no people about. "I wanted to ask you if Michael had talked you into becoming a Fenian. He can be very persuasive, can't he?" she whispered.

James went very quiet. It was uncanny how well they could read each other, most of the time it was a good thing. At that moment, James was unsure of how he truly felt.

"I will admit to being sympathetic to Michael's cause and if I was a single man, with no responsibilities, I could have been easily persuaded by him. I was surprised that he never even tried to talk me into some sort of fund raising at least, but he didn't, Mary. So you can rest assured that I won't be bringing any trouble to our door on that account. Michael is driven by something deep inside of him. When we said goodbye I felt as if I was

202

walking away from the loneliest man in the world."

"Sure how could Michael be lonely? He has Brigid and a houseful of children and lodgers, hasn't he?" asked Mary.

"I know, love. I was probably imagining it. It was sad parting from him, not knowing if we would ever meet again."

"Who knows what might happen in the future? Look at us, money in the bank in Ardee, waiting for our return. A fine brood of children to keep us on our toes. Three regular wages coming into the house. We have a lot to be thankful for, haven't we, James? Can you not find happiness in any of that?"

It was the right thing to say to him and it pulled James out of a sadness that had been hanging over him, ever since his meeting with Michael. Their future did look hopeful. He knew they would face any troubles that lay ahead exactly the same way as they had done in the past, with determination and perseverance. James saw the anxiety on his wife's face and kissed the creases on her forehead.

"Don't worry, Mary. As long as I have you and the children I have more than enough reason to be happy. Come on, we should be getting back to the house before all the food is gone."

James and Mary walked arm in arm back to where the sound of a party was in full swing, spilling music and laughter into the street. As they stepped over the threshold of the door and into the midst of their family, James was caught up in the merriment and laughter. It wasn't the hot stove that caused the warmth he felt inside him. Nor was it the crowded bodies happily squashed into such a tiny space. It was the feeling of home. James looked around the smiling faces and realized he had been home all along.

"Mary," he shouted above the music coming from his brother's fiddle, "This is home."

"I know, James. I know it is. For now at least and sure isn't that . . ." Mary's words trailed off as they were both sucked into a set to dance the *Walls of Limerick.*

THE END

REFERENCES

Mamó and Dadó

Titles sometimes used by Irish grandchildren in times past for Grandmother and Grandfather.

The Mary Stoddart

On Tuesday 6th April 1858, the *Mary Stoddart* a low hulled barque that sailed from Scarborough, broke anchor in a storm in Dundalk Bay and ran aground between Soldier's Point and Blackrock. Onlookers on the shore could see the crew hanging onto the rigging, as the ship's decks were two to three feet below high tide. When repeated attempts to rescue the men failed, due to the violent storm that raged, the crew on the *Mary Stoddart* spent the next few days tied to the masts while further attempts were made to save them.

Three days later, on a Friday morning, Captains Kelly and Hinds attempted another rescue, but Kelly's boat overturned and he and one of the men, James Murphy, drowned. Captain Hinds, whose boat was also unable to reach the *Mary Stoddart*, lifted the surviving members of Kelly's crew out of the water but one of them, Gerald Hughes, died on the way back to shore. All of the men were suffering from exposure and exhaustion. James Crosbey aged 25, died in a local woman's house not long afterwards.

Nine men died altogether, five on the ship and the above mentioned four in the rescue attempt.

The following year a lifeboat house was established at Blackrock, funded by Lord Clermont.

(From *The Parish of Haggardstown and Blackrock a History* by Noel Sharkey).

Malcolm Brown Distillery Dundalk 1800-1925

The distillery was established in 1800 by Messrs James Gillichan and Peter Goodbey and changed hands many times until its closure in 1925.

It was not only famous for its whiskey. In 1817 the company, which had changed its name to Malcolm Brown, built a great chimney, said to be the tallest one in Ireland at the time. It was 24ft sq. at its base, 14ft sq. at the top and 162ft high. It was built that high for economic reasons - at the time alcohol duty was calculated on the length of time a pot still was working, so by building a very high chimney, Malcolm Brown could have the firing completed in as short a time as possible. The regulations were changed in 1823, when duty was calculated on the quantity of spirits distilled, and the chimney came to be known as *"Brown's Folly"*. This chimney not only became the principal landmark within miles of Dundalk, but it was also used by sailors as a leading navigational aid for over 100 years.

(From *The Ireland Whiskey Trail* www.irelandwhiskeytrail.com)

The Young Irelanders and The Fenians

For a history of the struggle for independence see www.libraryireland.com